D0840050

Can Every
School Succeed?

PRAISE FOR *CAN EVERY SCHOOL SUCCEED?*

"A line has been drawn in the sand. No longer is there a middle ground. Schools must make a choice: to embrace or resist change (transformation). To either be progressive in their approaches and programs or stagnant. To either be responsive to the needs of their students or to maintain the status quo." —**Dr. Wade D. Steinhoff**, assistant superintendent, Orchard Farm R-V School District, Orchard Farm, MO

"For today's learners to succeed they must be more than engaged. They must be empowered. This creates an urgent need for schools to provide personalized and challenging learning experiences to meet the needs of each learner. Only by responding to the individual needs of our students can our schools truly be transformed." —**Klista Rader,** teacher and curriculum director, Lockwood R-1 Public Schools, Lockwood, MO

"Our work with school leadership development across multiple continents has yielded many significant patterns and findings, but one in particular is as striking as it is global across all education systems: the schools willing to challenge existing post-industrial educational paradigms, embrace the future as now, and make transformation and change their driving vision and mission, are the schools achieving by far the most exciting, meaningful, and resonant outcomes for their students. In order to most effectively lead their learners they are learning to lead themselves—into brave new territories." —**Jason D. Renshaw**, chief learning innovation officer, National Excellence in School Leadership Initiative

Can Every School Succeed?

Bending Constructs to Transform an American Icon

Brian Creasman, Jesse Bacon,
and David Franklin

ROWMAN & LITTLEFIELD
Lanham • Boulder • New York • London

Published by Rowman & Littlefield
A wholly owned subsidiary of The Rowman & Littlefield Publishing Group, Inc.
4501 Forbes Boulevard, Suite 200, Lanham, Maryland 20706
www.rowman.com

Unit A, Whitacre Mews, 26-34 Stannary Street, London SE11 4AB

Copyright © 2018 by Brian Creasman, Jesse Bacon, and David Franklin

All rights reserved. No part of this book may be reproduced in any form or by any electronic or mechanical means, including information storage and retrieval systems, without written permission from the publisher, except by a reviewer who may quote passages in a review.

British Library Cataloguing in Publication Information Available

Library of Congress Cataloging-in-Publication Data

Names: Creasman, Brian, author.
Title: Can every school succeed? : bending constructs to transform an American icon / by Brian Creasman, Jesse Bacon, and David Franklin.
Description: Lanham : Rowman & Littlefield, [2017] | Includes bibliographical references.
Identifiers: LCCN 2017060143 (print) | LCCN 2018002709 (ebook) | ISBN 9781475840605 (electronic) | ISBN 9781475840582 (cloth : alk. paper) | ISBN 9781475840599 (pbk. : alk. paper)
Subjects: LCSH: School improvement programs—United States.
Classification: LCC LB2822.82 (ebook) | LCC LB2822.82 .C73 2017 (print) | DDC 371.2/07—dc23
LC record available at https://lccn.loc.gov/2017060143

∞™ The paper used in this publication meets the minimum requirements of American National Standard for Information Sciences—Permanence of Paper for Printed Library Materials, ANSI/NISO Z39.48-1992.

Printed in the United States of America

Contents

Foreword vii

Preface ix

Acknowledgments xiii

Introduction xvii

Setting the Stage: Can Every School Succeed? xxi

1 Vision: Finding Your School's Identity 1

2 Journey: Preparing for an Epic Blastoff 23

3 Buy-In: Strengthening Opportunities for Success through Engagement 43

4 Empowerment: Increasing Social Capital through Collaboration 59

5 Change: Creating a School Students Need and Want 73

6 Capacity: Building Structures for New Forms of Leadership 91

7 Execution: Implementing the Strategy 107

8 Sustainability: Going Beyond Tomorow 125

Conclusion 141

Afterword 145

Bibliography 147

About the Authors 151

Foreword

Leadership is often a term associated with titles and authority. People in leadership roles can be placed in situations where they are the sole decision maker, and it is lonely. Some may prefer being alone at the top, leading complex organizations; however, the longevity of isolated leaders is very short. Top down leadership exists, but is ultimately harmful to the people involved. Leaders are incapable of transforming schools into organizations *for* kids if they do not provide an inclusive vision. Our kids deserve more than leaders in silos (insert excitable and passionate voice)! Our kids deserve leaders who serve as vision champions and catalysts for transformational change.

When I was first shown the eight principles of school transformation in *Can Every School Succeed?*, I found myself thinking, "Wow! Why didn't I think of this?" They are simplistic in nature, but take a plethora of dedication, passion, and persistence. Leading is messy. It just is! There is no handbook or manual on how to lead a school. It takes much more than years of teaching experience and pedagogy. Transformative leaders pull others in with their voracious passion and commitment to what is best for students.

They are transparent about their need for support, because they cannot be a vision champion alone! Their hunger and desire to strive for greatness is infectious, and causes others to want what they have. Transformation is a journey on which every school must embark. Mediocre schools are led by mediocre people, and will not become better for kids until the people have a roadmap. We want to know where we are headed, and we need to have a plan to get there.

Will there be side roads, bumps, and wrong turns? Absolutely! The visionary leader will serve as the navigator, along with a team who shares in decisions along the way. Throughout the journey, these people evolve, become empowered, and execute what is necessary in order to sustain a steady path toward excellence. A transformative leader will make change nonnegotiable, but will not forget what is most important . . . the people.

As a lead learner, I always filter ideas and decisions through "The Three P's": purpose, passion, and persistence. As leaders who strive to transform and sustain schools of excellence, we always start with the purpose (why we do what we do). We then use our passion to express joy, fulfillment, and hunger to live in the now, but envision what our kids need to be future ready. Passionate leaders empower and ignite others to move forward with us!

As a team we persist through the challenges, barriers, and mandates in order to keep our vision in sight. Leaders, we cannot lead alone. Our goal is student success, and we owe it to our kids to serve them as transformative teams who continue to strive for excellence. We do not give up. We are vision champions. *We.* When *we* commit to creating a school for students, *they* . . . the students *win*!

Bethany Hill
Lead Learner, Central Elementary
Cabot, Arkansas

Preface

"Greatness is not a function of circumstance. Greatness, it turns out, is largely a matter of conscious choice, and discipline."

—John C. Collins

GOOD TO GREAT: WHY SOME COMPANIES MAKE THE LEAP . . . AND OTHERS DON'T

So you have recently been named principal of a school—congratulations! There are few jobs more challenging, as this role has become increasingly more difficult over the last several years. However, there are few jobs more rewarding. When you are named principal for the first time, or perhaps you are named principal of a new school, you immediately begin to think about next steps. What unique skills and experiences do I bring to the table?

What specific steps do I need to take to help the staff transform a good school or even a not-so-good school to create a "great" school? What value will I bring to the students, staff, and community? There are lots of directions to go and many obstacles waiting ahead. However, you can't do it alone. Fortunately, help is on the way! It is well documented that the school principal is critical to the success of any school. Being selected to serve as a principal for a school is quite an honor. You were ultimately selected to serve in this capacity for many good reasons.

Obviously, your past success has led you to achieve this important milestone in your career. However, the real challenge comes when a new leader faces the task of moving a school to the next level. Sometimes, this realization comes to you even after you have served in your current role for a period of time. Clearly, you were not placed in this essential position to maintain the status quo. If you do, you will most likely not serve in that capacity for long.

Ultimately, as a principal, you want your students and your school to be successful. However, success can be defined in many ways. It is unfortunate that many of our schools, and even our success as school leaders, are defined solely by state test scores. As a principal, you need to work with your staff to expand your thinking to define what success looks like. We must remember that when students succeed, we succeed as school leaders, teachers, and staff members.

The authors of *Can Every School Succeed?: Bending Constructs to Transform an American Icon* appropriately lead the reader to this realization in the first chapter, which is focused on setting a vision for the school. This requires the staff working together to create a clear and inspiring vision that will guide the path for the future. With that, your school transformation journey begins! Each chapter provides principles important to success, while guiding the school leader toward successful change implementation and sustainability. The chapters are simple and can be used by novice or veteran school leaders to begin to transform their schools.

In *Can Every School Succeed?* you will be guided through a series of key principles to effectively navigate the change process required to move a school from good to great. The text is well-supported by research related to school leadership and successful change implementation. Each chapter includes tried and true strategies that any leader can implement immediately. However, this powerful text does not stop there. It also includes practical, actionable examples as well as voices from leaders in the field through notable quotes included in each chapter.

Whether you are a new principal, newly assigned to a building, or even an existing principal who wants to shepherd your school to the next level, this is a powerful resource for you. There are several reasons to read *Can Every School Succeed?* One is that it inspires hope to school leaders who have a passion for providing the best possible learning experiences for their students.

Leaders who see students as more than test scores. Leaders who understand the moral imperative we face as school leaders and that it is our job to do much more than prepare students for a state test. In addition, this text provides a wealth of research and examples of school transformation in a hands-on, predictable format for readers to follow. *Can Every School Succeed?* also provides concrete, practical examples to follow as you work with school staff to implement lasting change in your school.

Relevant vignettes are also provided through Principal's Notes in order to provide real-life examples of the exciting work ahead. Finally, the reader is encouraged to take advantage of powerful opportunities to reflect on his or her own practice. Indeed, this will lead to improved leadership success! School leaders must always look for blueprints, maps, and frameworks that can improve their effectiveness, like *Can Every School Succeed?*

It won't be easy. However, *Can Every School Succeed?* will equip you with the tools needed to take student learning, engagement, and success to the next level. Isn't that what school is all about? It is time for all of us to come together to create the school our students deserve. We must always remember that schools are about students—creating the best opportunities that will lead to their success.

> Dr. Jared A. Cotton
> Superintendent
> Henry County Schools, Virginia

Acknowledgments

Today's schools are dynamic organizations that unfortunately are only becoming more complex each day. Your work as a school leader, teacher, or staff member is commended and admirable. You are indeed in the most important profession in the world, even though today's educators rarely receive the recognition that we deserve. Our work today charts the future for the nation and tomorrow's nurses, doctors, lawyers, and leaders.

What we do today does impact the future; therefore, our work cannot be undervalued—especially as students' needs, goals, and aspirations continue to expand and diversify. As the Every Student Succeeds Act (ESSA) becomes the law of the land and is implemented in schools across the nation, we felt it was pertinent to revisit the idea of school transformation and pose the question *Can Every School Succeed*?

In our opinion and based on our experience, we believe every school can succeed, as there are remarkable school leaders, teachers, and staff members who are working tirelessly to ensure that every student achieves success. Time and time again, we have tried to convey the importance of understanding that the only way schools succeed is if students succeed. In our opinion, too many educators forget or overlook how student success is forever interconnected with school success.

We feel that when everyone has a laser focus on student success, schools will eventually succeed. Over our careers as school administrators, we have been fortunate to have worked with and met some of the best leaders, teachers, and staff members. It is through these experiences and interactions that we have ultimately shaped our thinking toward school transformation. Each day, we see remarkable things that school administrators, teachers, and staff members are doing that transform the lives of students.

From personalizing a worksheet for a student, having lunch with a student who sits alone in the cafeteria, to purchasing a bookbag or clothes for students, we see transformation each day. These experiences are not only rewarding but also transformative to students and schools. We believe this work is a calling, not a job. To create the transformation that is needed to help all students succeed, school leaders and educators must view the work through the lens of urgency and a higher calling to lead, teach, and change.

Our students today are better prepared and equipped to enter college, the workforce, and for life than at any other time in modern history. The reason is because of the work that school leaders, teachers, and staff members perform each day. Their work is strengthened by their commitment to their students—which we recognize, salute, and for which we offer a heartfelt thank you. *Can Every School Succeed?: Bending Constructs to Transform an American Icon* is the result of numerous and lengthy brainstorming sessions, rough drafts, and discussions. More importantly, we would not have been able to bring the book to fruition if not for the help of many.

We want to thank Bethany Hill for writing a spectacular foreword. Her role as a positive, high-energy, transformative school leader brought a certain level of positivity to the book, which was perfect. Her foreword provided the needed foundation for the reader. We decided to have the preface written by Jared Cotton, a nationally recognized, innovative school superintendent that has transformed a school district through the use of technology and personalized learning. His experience and addition to our book is remarkable and provides credence to the need to transform schools into learning institutions focused on the individual student.

The afterword written by Randy Poe, also a nationally recognized school superintendent for his transformative work, focused on expanding instructional programing, support services and the power of positivity throughout the learning process, was an excellent ending to the book, but also a starting point for the reader to begin the transformation process in their school. Combined, Bethany's, Jared's, and Randy's additions provide a glimpse into what effective transformative leaders do each day—we encourage you to learn from them as we have and do each day.

We are fortunate to have the support and endorsements from nationally recognized leaders. We cannot thank Mike Lublefield, Nick Polyak, Jethro Jones, and Renee Gordon enough for their endorsements. All four are doing amazing things in schools today and are transformative in their work as leaders in education and human capital. They were supportive from the beginning as we put our thoughts to paper to offer current and aspiring change agents a roadmap to transforming schools. We cannot say thank you enough for your support.

But ultimately we have to thank our families who allowed us the time to focus on this critical work in the realm of education. The three of us believe education is the most important and rewarding work in the world today. As such, we have to make sure that we get education right today so that our children's futures remain bright and prosperous. Our families support encourages us and gives us the fuel to persist through challenges, setbacks, and failure. Thank you!

Introduction

THE TRANSFORMATIVE PRINCIPLES

The ultimate goal of *Can Every School Succeed?* is to remain simple to read and understand, so as not to add to the complexities of school transformation. The overall process of transformation, to be successful, needs to be simple to understand and implement. At the beginning of each chapter, the reader will notice the figure below, indicating where they are in the transformation process that is presented.

The figure is simple to understand and will help school leaders, teachers, and staff members to keep track of their progress as they begin critical change processes in their schools. The figure can be used to help keep other school stakeholders, such as parents, community members, and business leaders up to speed about where the school is in regards to transformation. The process that is presented is simple to follow and can be used in schools, as a constant reminder of where the school is at and where it is going throughout the transformation process.

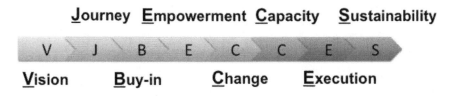

Through our experience as experienced school administrators in California, Kentucky, and North Carolina, we have collectively identified key components that form the basis for school transformation. Our experiences are diverse, ranging from rural and urban schools; elementary, middle, and high schools; and education systems in different states. No matter the size, location, or configuration, most all school transformation utilizes the principles that we provide in our book.

For some, much of the information will sound familiar; for others, the principles will be new and different. After the image is presented, an explanation of each principle is provided in relevant and concise terms that will help school leaders initiate a remarkable and transformative journey. We encourage school leaders, teachers, and staff members to blow up the image and post it throughout their school, in workrooms, in classrooms, and in professional learning spaces.

HOW THE BOOK IS ORGANIZED

Transformative Core Idea

The transformative core idea provides the overarching importance of the principle presented. The principle is defined in practical terms: why transformation is needed and how the principle fits into the change process. The goal is to keep the transformative core idea concise to provide school leaders with information to easily analyze and share with others. The ideas presented are provided to encourage school leaders to picture the school through a different lens: what students need and expect. Embracing student needs and expectations is vision critical to the long-term success of schools that wish to remain relevant in today's crowded educational landscape.

Transformative Key Understandings

The transformative key understandings are provided to provide the change process in practical terms. The key understandings provide school leaders foundational information that can help school leaders lead transformation effectively. The information presented in this section will help school leaders to determine the roles of stakeholders throughout the process. Too often, school leaders, teachers, and staff members lack an understanding of transformation, which stops their school from ever beginning the critical process of changing processes, structures, and protocols.

Transformative Roles

The transformative roles section provides a clear definition of the roles for school leaders, teachers, and staff members, as transformation is the responsibility of all stakeholders in the school. This is distinctive, as most books pertaining to school transformation do not delineate the roles as we have, nor do other books encourage the empowerment of stakeholders to be leaders throughout the transformation. Each team member needs to know his or her role as the school begins the transformation process. Each role is critical to growing the capacity for the school to change and sustaining the work that occurs.

Research and Transformation

The research and transformation section helps to provide validity to the transformation process. The section offers academic research in concise and practical terms that will help the reader to understand the transformation process, removing any barriers to the beginning of the change process. As schools begin the transformation process, understanding the basis for change is essential to obtaining support from stakeholders. Stakeholders are more willing to support change when the processes are backed by research.

Transformative Points to Consider

The transformative points to consider section is meant to be used by the reader as a quick reference guide. Through our networks, personal experiences, professional friendships, and one-on-one conversations, we have developed these powerful transformative key points. Each point speaks to the practical nature of the transformative principles presented, and serves as a guide to school leaders who choose to begin the transformation process in their schools. The transformative points add validation to the need for schools to change to meet the growing, diversifying needs of students.

TransformED

The TransformED section provides relevant information and understanding about the transformation process. The transformation terms, such as vision, journey, and other principles are inserted before the TransformED section in each chapter. The TransformED section is meant to inspire school leaders to begin the process. Embedded into each section are practical experiences and strategies that will help school leaders to understand the transformation process better, and to better understand each principle. Unlike in most books, the TransformED section is free from counterproductive educational jargon that typically leads to more confusion.

Transformative Ideas from the Field

The transformative ideas from the field section is for final considerations for each principle. This section is meant to serve as a differing viewpoint about the transformation process that will help strengthen the reader's understanding about the principle and better position the school leader to be an effective change agent. The information is presented to encourage school leaders, teachers, and staff members to begin a conversation about transformation at their school. The goal is to use the ideas from the field as a means to strategically create a transformation process that targets the school's diverse needs and goals.

Principal's Notes

The principal's notes are a fascinating, practical, and real transformative vignette. This section provides school leaders a short example of how the particular transformative principle may look in their school. The reader is given a glimpse into the transformation process as it took place at Spring Water Elementary School. The reader is provided a scenario that the principal at Spring Water Elementary School experienced throughout the change process. The best way to gain an understanding of each principle of the transformation process is to see how a real school administrator led the change process and how the transformation may look in another school.

Takeaway Ideas

The takeaway ideas section is a very important section for a couple of different reasons. (1) The section is meant to offer key advice to school leaders at they begin the transformation process. (2) The section will help to identify possible obstacles that leaders will need to overcome throughout the transformative journey. (3) The takeaway idea serves as a summary of each chapter. The section connects the principle to the following principle so that the transformation process remains simple, smooth, and connected.

Setting the Stage

Can Every School Succeed?

"If the rate of change outside your organization is greater than the rate of change inside your organization, then the end is in sight."

—Jack Welch

Schools are facing incredible challenges. *Within the next three to five years, many, if not all school leaders will be competing with outside learning organizations based on student experience.* There is a growing and urgent need for public schools, an American icon, to bend constructs to engage students in the learning process differently. Students want schools to be centers of inspiration, personalized to their needs, goals, and aspirations. The time for educating to the masses, using cookie-cutter approaches to educating students, is effectively over.

Schools have reached the crossroads and must become student-focused to remain relevant in the teaching and learning process. Think about all of the complexities that face school leaders today: stagnant or decreasing school budgets, increasing teacher and administrator turnover, and increasing accountability requirements. As the complexities continue to increase, the school as an organization must recognize the need to change, to transform.

Change is no longer optional, as students and parents now have a buffet of options to choose from: public education, private education, charter education, home school, and online education. The traditional public school that every community has is no longer the only school in town, and students and parents realize this. In the past, schools did not have to cater to the needs of students, as the competition was few to nonexistent. That is no longer the case today.

School leaders are responsible for creating and communicating the urgency for change to occur. To do so, they, school leaders, must recognize that change is critical to long-term success of the school and for students. Just as academic programs change regularly, school structures and organization must also change. It is this change that allows schools and school districts to remain a relevant force in helping students succeed. Though schools are facing an uphill battle to change, the change process can be a remarkable, transformative if you will, journey.

Public schools today are the result of almost a century worth of changes, policies, and reform efforts. What many of our students experience each day is the product of work that was done during a time when schools had little to no pressure to succeed. Unfortunately, this means that many of our schools today are using models that are outdated, irrelevant, and nowhere close to meeting the needs of our students.

Now, to be clear, there are many schools today that are doing phenomenal work in preparing students for the next level of education. Those particular schools have embraced change as a means to introduce new and cutting-edge opportunities such as dual-credit programs, personalized learning, open classrooms, work-based/apprentice programs, and many others.

Those schools that are high performing provide other schools an excellent model of transformation. Yes, those schools at some point began the change process that has ultimately led to their success. Now, they may refer to their transformation as something other than transformation. Nevertheless, they went through a strategic change process to transform the school's culture, structures, leadership, and overall purpose.

In other words, they "bent constructs" to remain relevant to students. Those schools understood that for their students to be prepared for tomorrow and competitive on the global stage, they needed to revamp their mission and vision. School leaders must recognize the challenges that accompany change. Throughout the transformation process, there will be some of the school's stakeholders who will challenge change, as they prefer not to leave their comfort zones.

The transformation process challenges school leaders to encourage others to push the limits and also to work together to help increase student achievement. Schools are complex organizations that require school leaders, teachers, and staff members working together, focused on the same vision, change, and more importantly increasing student achievement.

Ultimately, the effectiveness of the transformation process will be determined by how well school leaders can get others to work together to challenge the status quo and leave their comfort zones. Sometimes transformation will seem like an art and not a science, as the school leader's skills will be worked in completely different ways throughout the change process.

BENDING CONSTRUCTS

"Transformation is often more about unlearning than learning."

—Richard Rohr

As practitioners and school leaders, we felt that discussing transformation in straightforward and concise terms would be more beneficial to those school leaders who decide to explore the transformation principles and process that we present throughout *Can Every School Succeed?: Bending Constructs to Transform an American Icon*. As authors we recognize the importance of basing our writing on theory and research; therefore, we provide this section to validate the basis of school transformation.

Relevant research helps to strengthen a leader's practical experience. Research lends critical background data that, if used, can strengthen the outcomes of school transformation. Though we would like to present transformation as a new process, we realize that school transformation has been around for decades. In many cases school transformation is referred to as school turnaround, school change, school restart, and many other terms.

Many times school transformation, as discussed in research, is presented in terms of school closure, replacing the school's principal, and the school being converted to a charter school. All of which are the results of No Child Left Behind and the intense focus on determining school success by student test results. As we try to convey throughout *Can Every School Succeed?* there are obviously other components in schools that need to be considered throughout the change process.

To be clear, we do not argue that school transformation be solely focused on student test results; however, test results remain a critical component to determining student success, unfortunately. The transformation model that we are presenting focuses heavily on transforming the school's organization, structures, vision, and leadership. According to Matveev and Lvina (2007), transformational leaders create change through effective communication and by focusing on the organization's vision.

Throughout *Can Every School Succeed?* the need for an inspiring vision is critical to each transformational principle. The vision for transformation, the ultimate goal of the change process, must be closely aligned to the overall school's vision, if not the same. Our basis for school transformation is closely aligned to the definition of a transformational leader.

According to Yukl (1999), transformational leaders encourage and inspire followers to reach higher expectations and to change their beliefs and values in regards to what they see as the purpose of school. As we try to convey vividly, vision is the driving force behind the transformation of any school, or any organization for that matter.

Schools can change or transform if the vision for change inspires change among stakeholders, particularly teachers, staff members, and the greater school community. School leaders are encouraged to rely heavily on the school's vision—to make changes that will lead to the greatest positive impact on student success. School transformation will only occur if the school's leader has the energy, charisma, and determination to lead the needed change.

But specifically, the school leader must have the belief that change can occur. Throughout the transformation process, the school leader will face obstacles, setbacks, and even challenges to their leadership (directly and indirectly). When a leader begins to challenge individuals' comfort zones, those individuals, most likely, will at first push back and then, ultimately, embrace the process.

Change, without question, is hard; however, if communicated to stakeholders in terms that are relevant to them, concisely, and in a way that is positive, not punitive, school leaders will be far more effective in helping to lead change in schools. The transformational model that we present throughout this book is aligned to Leithwood and Jantzi (2006), which requires that school leaders set the direction (vision), lead the development of people, lead the redesign of the organization, and lead the improvements of the teaching and learning process.

Throughout this book, the concepts that Leithwood and Jantzi highlight are found embedded into the eight transformative principles that form the basis of the transformational model that is proposed in *Can Every School Succeed*. School leaders are encouraged to view transformation as a continual and developmental process that will be determined by the real-time needs of students. Schools must change as the needs, goals, and aspirations of students change—though this is possibly a new and daunting task for many schools, ultimately, schools must change in order to succeed.

A difference in our transformational model is that each principle encourages a new way of thinking in schools. For decades, all school leaders continued to convey the need for schools to change to meet twenty-first-century expectations. As we are now seventeen years into the twenty-first century, we submit that we must now begin to rethink our schools and prepare for the twenty-second century.

The majority of schools are still constrained, not to a twenty-first-century model, but to a twentieth-century model of education—when education was for the masses and was not focused on the needs and interests of each student. Schools have become a victim of their own system. Constructs should never stand in the way of student success or impede progress or change. All schools, based on what students today expect, must be more about the student and less about structures.

We challenge school leaders, teachers, and staff members to transform schools so that there is a focus on all students. With pressures mounting for students to be college and career ready, and for schools to close the achievement gap, schools must become learning centers that are focused on the needs, goals, and aspirations of all students. Today's schools must transform; if they do not, the achievement gap will only widen.

The need to change has never been greater. Schools must become centers of learning for all students if they expect to succeed. School structures are those organizational, operational, instructional, and cultural components found in all schools. To be exact, we are speaking specifically about bell schedules, instructional processes, accountability requirements, organizational charts, and student support systems, just to mention a few. School leaders, teachers, and staff members working together must be willing to transform any structure that is impeding ALL students from succeeding. The formation of the school structures did not occur overnight, they formed over time, and, as such, changing those structures will take time. Though structures are important in schools, the need to ensure all students succeed far outweighs the need to remain restricted by constructs that may impede student success. No school ever fails when school leaders, teachers, and staff members have a "do whatever it takes" mentality to ensuring students succeed.

THE FOUNDATION OF THE
TRANSFORMATION PRINCIPLES

"The secret of change is to focus all of your energy, not on fighting the old, but on building the new."

—Socrates

There are countless books that focus on some form of school transformation. *Can Every School Succeed?* provides current and aspiring school leaders components that have been collected and utilized over the years. Collectively, each component is essential to transforming the school's many processes, particularly the teaching and learning process.

In practical terms, school transformation is a situational change process, a process that is constantly evolving as a result of changes in student demographics, academic needs, teacher turnover, and even shifts in the school administration. Nevertheless, the essential components of the transformation process help to form the foundation necessary to create lasting change within the school.

Can Every School Succeed? can help practitioners begin a very challenging process. Few school leaders and schools nationwide choose to start the transformation process. The reluctance of school leaders, teachers, and staff members, unfortunately, is impeding the success of students. Today's schools must become more student-centered and less structure-centered.

Instead of challenging change, school leaders, teachers, and staff members must be willing to push the boundaries of the teaching and learning process. As such, school leaders and educators are focused more on doing whatever it takes to meet the needs of students than being restricted by their structures and protocols. Schools have become victimized by the very systems and structures that once were developed to help students. However, in many of today's schools, there is more focus on doing what is most comfortable for adults than doing what is best for students.

Can Every School Succeed? encourages school leaders to challenge the status quo and help others push the boundaries of the teaching and learning process. Today's teachers, staff, and students need visionary school leaders who are willing to serve others, help others to achieve higher levels of excellence, and know how to engage others in the change process.

Change is not easy, neither is creating a culture based on a collaborative, shared decision-making process. Collaboration and shared decision-making are pillars of school transformation; both lead to engagement and empowerment. School leaders need an army of teachers and staff members who want to be leaders in school, ready to step up to the plate and to help ensure that the transformation process results in improved student success, improved teacher and school leader effectiveness, and school-wide change.

Throughout the transformation process, there will always be opportunities to make improvements. As obstacles, setbacks, and barriers appear, school leaders must be prepared to make improvements so that the smallest obstacle does not derail the entire transformative journey. Furthermore, as the process begins and the results fail to meet the common expectations of the team, school leaders must be prepared to make course corrections—which is perfectly acceptable.

The key is to communicate why changes in the journey are needed to remain aligned to the school's vision and vision for change. Communicating in terms of inspiration and hope, instead of fear and despiration, can help many embrace change by casting it in positive terms. School leaders, teachers, and staff members have an opportunity to do something amazing for students—create schools that are focused solely on their success and preparedness for the next level.

The transformation process helps to encourage school leaders, teachers, and staff members to push the boundaries of the teaching and learning process, while they take risks that will result in phenomenal growth for students, and also lead to personalized learning experiences. The change that is needed will take visionary leaders, teachers, and staff members who understand, support, and commit to creating a learning organization that is focused and strategic in meeting the needs, goals, and dreams of students.

Ultimately, the effectiveness of the transformation process will be measured not by an achievement score, but by the success of students to be college-, career-, and life-ready. Student success must always be the goal of school transformation. As schools are already complex organizations with mounting pressures to succeed, the transformation process must remain simple in implementation.

The transformation journey will be challenging, which is why the transformative message and plan implementation must be simple—free from much of the educational jargon that sometimes derails even the best plans—specifically the transformation process. The need for leaders who communicate effectively will be vision critical.

Effectively communicating the journey, the challenges, and progress will help to simplify the change process and keep the focus on student success. In relevant terms, simplicity should not be mistaken for lowered expectations. Simplicity only means keeping the change process clear, consistent, and easy to understand—while maintaining high expectations for student success.

Schools today must become centers of success for ALL students. In essence, the motto of all schools must become "do whatever it takes so ALL students succeed." Schools today need to succeed more now than at any time before, as the charter, private, and homeschool movements are increasingly becoming more appealing to students and parents. The reason is that there are less constructs that impede student success or there is a school culture focused on students, not adults.

Schools today need to be urgently transformed into places where students are encouraged to take risks, to push the boundaries of their learning, and to dream. In every sense, schools must become "student success mills" pumping out students who are prepared for college, career, and life. The more schools become focused on ensuring the success of ALL students, the more transformative the results will be for students.

For students to aspire to be great, schools must inspire imagination, creativity, and risk-taking, all of which have fallen by the wayside in the majority of schools today. School leaders, teachers, and staff members know what needs to be done; the transformation process only validates and gives credence to the decision to "do whatever it takes" to ensure student success and preparedness for the next level.

Chances to transform schools and to create long-term structural changes are scarce. If the opportunity exists for transformation to happen, school leaders must embrace the opportunity to do something great for students and the school. Change is not isolated to only low-performing schools. High-performing schools can improve just as much as low-performing schools.

The message is: if the opportunity presents itself, school leaders must encourage teachers and staff members to embrace a chance to help increase opportunities for students and create a culture that is more student-centered. School transformation is not an easy process. School transformation requires the assistance of transformative leaders who are willing to go the extra mile to ensure all students experience success and that the school's structures are conducive to this success.

Often, school transformation is viewed as a cyclical process. In other words, school transformation is a process that has no finish line. Based on our experience as school administrators, we view school and district transformation as an ongoing process, a journey with no destination. Though transformation may not have a destination, some specific components and benchmarks are commonly used throughout the process.

School and district transformation must always begin with a clear, laser focus on the actual work of ensuring student success. School and district personnel must understand that their inherent job and responsibility is to ensure all students are successful. Far too often, teachers, schools, and school administrators view student success as separate from school and district success.

Schools are incapable of being successful without students experiencing success. The two, student success and organizational success, are forever forged together and it is imperative that school and district leaders understand this. Through transformation, schools and districts are focused on reaching certain benchmarks and must continually focus on improving.

Transformation, no matter if it is at the school or district level, is always about continuously improving to meet the ever-changing needs of students. Again, this is why transformation never truly has a destination, but instead has benchmarks along a powerful and empowering journey. Through the continuous improvement process, the transformation process is strengthened and becomes more relevant to the needs and goals of the school and district.

For transformation to be successful, the school and district's culture must be conducive to continuous improvement. Creating a culture of continuous improvement improves the ability of transformative processes and practices to "take root" in the organizational structures and processes. As mentioned, the transformation process is never really finished; school and district leaders must continually monitor, correct, and improve the overall process.

Chapter One

Vision

Finding Your School's Identity

Many view school transformation as a process that is too daunting to begin or finish. Visionary school leaders realize the positives for students, teachers, staff members, the school, and the greater school community. School leaders and staff members must be brave enough to believe in their ideas and be willing to follow their dreams in order to take the first step in the transformation process. The end results may be hard to imagine, to describe, and communicate for school leaders, but they see it and must invite others to be part of the process and help them to see the possibilities.

School leaders recognize that no change is too big or small on the journey to creating a student-centered learning organization. Transformation challenges the notion of standardization, by suggesting that schools should have no boundaries or limits in creating the best learning organization and environment for students.

TRANSFORMATION CORE IDEA

School transformation will not occur unless the process is aligned to the school's overall vision. Furthermore, the vision for change must be inspiring, aligned, and adaptable to the needs of the school, students, and teachers.

The school's vision must be the driving force of the transformation process. Therefore, both the vision for the transformation process and the school must be interconnected. In other words, each vision should be one and the same and must work together to drive school change. Also, both the school vision and vision for transformation must be focused solely on creating the best opportunities, developing and implementing the best learning programs that will lead to student success. However, the greatest impact on student success is based on the effectiveness of teaching in the classroom.

TRANSFORMATIVE KEY UNDERSTANDINGS

- *Collaborative*—a school vision created through collaboration.
- *Inspiring*—the vision inspires others to be part of the school and change process.
- *Continuous Improvement*—the vision challenges school leaders, teachers, and staff members to continually seek opportunities to improve for students.
- *Focused*—the vision is focused on student success.
- *Challenging*—the vision challenges stakeholders to be creative, to take risks, to push the boundaries of the teaching and learning process to reach new, higher levels of student success and professional effectiveness.
- *Goal-oriented*—the vision is simple, uniting, and used by all to make school-wide decisions.

TRANSFORMATIVE ROLES

School Leaders:

- Communicate the school's vision;
- Assist others to understand the vision's components;
- Develop a team to help implement the school's vision;
- Engage diverse perspectives in developing the school's vision, and ensure that students are the focus and also involved in creating the school's vision.

Teachers and Staff Members:

- Engage in the development of the school's vision;
- Offer insights and experiences in an effort to strengthen the school's vision;
- Seek opportunities to participate in the development, implementation, and evaluation of the school's vision;
- Assist in aligning the teaching and learning process to the school's vision.

RESEARCH AND TRANSFORMATION

According to Kotter (1997), a vision gives the organization a picture of the future. To begin the transformation process, school leaders must clearly and concisely explain why the school needs a vision not only for day-to-day operations, but also for the transformation process. Why exactly is the school going through the transformation process? The best journeys are often derailed because the leader fails to communicate a goal or the purpose of the journey.

By starting the transformation with a vision for change, school leaders can, throughout the process, refer stakeholders back to the goals as obstacles develop or setbacks occur. If created with simplicity in mind, the vision can, and often will, put the "train back on the tracks" when challenges appear. Huffman and Hipp (2001) indicate that the central task of a school leader is to create a shared vision around a common task.

Rarely does school transformation begin in the absence of the school leader. In fact, we cannot find in research where school transformation begins without a school leader. The primary responsibility of the school leader is, in fact, to make sure that the vision for the school and transformation align to create a school culture, environment, and learning program that focuses on student success.

As educational leaders, we recognize that this is easier said than done; however, we feel that if the visioning process is done with fidelity, collaboratively, and in the open, then what is best for students will ultimately be the result. One final point of emphasis about school visions is conveyed by Schneider, Brief, and Guzzo (1996). The authors emphasize that vision statements need to be inspiring—especially if leaders expect to change the behavior of employees.

We encourage all school leaders to lead the development of vision statements that inspire the school stakeholders to aspire to be great and to seek to grow and change continuously. The vision for the school and transformation must be interconnected, as both help the school to meet the needs of students.

TRANSFORMATIVE POINTS TO CONSIDER

- Having a vision for school change starts with the school leader becoming a change agent and inspiring others to follow them.
- As schools begin the transformation process, it is obviously clear that without a vision, the stakeholders in the building will never change.

- Before schools change, the school must have a visionary leader that dares others to reach for the stars and is there to catch them if they fall.
- School principals must always start with the question, why is change needed? If the answer is about providing students the opportunities for success, you are on the right track. If the answer has nothing to do with students, go back to the drawing board—because change will not happen.

PRACTICAL INTRODUCTION

School transformation requires a clear vision. What is the purpose of school transformation in the context of creating the best learning institution for student success? Without a clear vision for the journey, school leaders will struggle with engaging stakeholders in the process. It is important that school leaders constantly communicate the school's vision—always relating all processes back to the school's vision. In fact, the school's vision must serve as the guiding principle for change.

For the transformation process to be effective, the vision for the school and transformation must be aligned. In other words, they are one and the same. Schools begin the transformation or change process as a means to meet the expectations of the school's vision. The school's vision must always challenge stakeholders to aspire to be something better for students. When developed by stakeholders collaboratively, the vision for the school and transformation process is a uniting force that can lead to improvements that will lead to increases in student success and preparedness for the next level.

Just as the school's vision must be inspiring to stakeholders, the vision for transformation must also inspire support and commitment to something bigger. Change, in any organization, is hard and will require an unwavering commitment by stakeholders—especially during setbacks, obstacles, and barriers. An effective, inspiring vision, coupled with a visionary leader, can help bring the best out of stakeholders as they ascend the proverbial mountain for students.

The vision for transformation must be communicated effectively, in a clear and simple manner, which will help stakeholders understand the mission and goals. By understanding the vision, stakeholders will be willing to push the boundaries and push through obstacles—if they believe in the change process. Stakeholders must understand how transformation not only leads to student success, but also how it impacts their roles in the school.

As educational leaders, how do we know if we have created a vision that that will motivate and inspire those we depend on? There seems to be almost universal agreement around the country that public education must change significantly. All we have to do is examine the political climate today to realize that legislators, parents, and even students are begging for a new vision for education. We can no longer simply dust off our richly written old statements about how our schools are all about helping students become productive citizens. We must create a new vision that transforms the way we go about educating our kids.

The problem that we continually run into is educators are not comfortable with creating a new vision. We are great at implementing new programs when given the components. However, creating a new vision? Most of us don't even know where to start. We must realize that true transformation is not about improving an existing product. Instead, it is about creating something totally new.

If we are serious about providing the type of education that will truly prepare students to lead our communities and our country into the next century, we must start to think differently. After all, most of our grandchildren will likely see the year 2100 (let that sink in for a minute). Yet we still use an educational model that was built in the late 1800s. True visionaries don't approach their work by simply polishing their existing organizations. Instead, visionary leaders are not concerned with rebuilding the school from ground up, touching every facet of the school in order to become student-centered.

All we need to do is look at some of the most successful companies in the world such as Apple, Amazon, and Starbucks to see examples of leaders who developed new and more efficient experiences for their customers. We must do the same for our students. To develop a new vision we must have a clear grasp on the experiences our students need everyday to achieve at high levels. We are starting to get a good understanding of that.

We know the benefits of meeting students at current levels, addressing different learning styles, presenting concepts and skills that are of high interest, providing opportunities for real world application, and assigning challenging and attainable tasks that, when completed, leave students excited about returning to school the next day. The problem with educational leaders is all too often we try and stuff the student learning experience into the current assembly-line structure of our public schools. Instead, we should ask ourselves, what do we have to do or create to make what our students believe is the most effective learning experience? In answering that question we must be prepared to offer that experience in ways that may not yet exist.

KEY QUESTIONS

The Key Questions are meant to help school leaders begin thinking about the transformation principles in relation to their schools.

- What is your school's vision?
- How is your school's vision related to school transformation?

- Discuss how your school's vision is student-centered, focused on student success.
- How will school transformation assist you in fulfilling the school's vision?

VISION TRANSFORMED

The starting point of all great journeys is actually the vision. In the case of schools, the vision is the navigator by which all decisions are made. All great organizations are guided by their vision and core beliefs. Schools are complex organizations with many moving parts. As of late, the complexities that face schools are only increasing as a result of stagnant or declining budgets, teacher turnover, changing student demographics, and increased accountability.

As such, the need to remain focused on the purpose of the teaching and learning process grows increasingly important. Student success must be the centerpiece of our vision. If we truly value the success of every student, our conversation must start with the learning experience that we provide. This is where reinvention begins. We need to follow the lead of some of the greatest visionaries of our time. There are examples of forward thinkers all around us that didn't just dust off and polish their organization's existing vision. Instead, they took a risk by reimagining the idea experience for their users and as a result, changed their respective industries forever.

This includes:

Apple's Steve Jobs;
Amazon's Jeff Bezos; and
Starbucks's Howard Shultz.

Very early in the school transformation process, school administrators must address the school's vision. The vision must be clearly communicated to all stakeholders, but more importantly, it must involve stakeholders. School administrators alone cannot create a vision that is engaging and empowering. Students, teachers, staff members, parents, and the community must have a voice in the development of the school vision.

Often, the development of a school vision is performed through face-to-face interviews or surveys. It is important for school leaders to utilize the best process that best fits their school. Each school will be different, which is why school administrators must utilize the vision process that will garner the best feedback and input from stakeholders. Diversity lends itself to creating a vision that can be embraced by all stakeholders.

The school's vision must be inspiring to all stakeholders, while also clearly communicating the expectations for all facets of the school process. No matter what, the school vision must be clearly understood by all stakeholders who are directly or indirectly connected to the school. It will be critically important that vision is in terms that everyone understands and supports. Here again, the more stakeholders are involved in creating the school's vision, the more likely they will understand the tenets of the vision and ultimately support the overall goals of the school.

Strategy: Be Vision Champions

> "Champions aren't made in gyms. Champions are made from something they have deep inside them: a desire, a dream, a vision!"
>
> —Muhammad Ali

School transformation requires some degree of a champion's spirit. The spirit that all professional athletes have—the willingness to never give up, the determination to win, and the persistence to be great. As schools begin the transformation process, it is important that school leaders, teachers, and staff members have a champion's mindset. Transformation is a change process with a purpose for creating the best learning environment and program for students.

The process will be rewarding to the team—school leaders, teachers, and staff members—if students experience success. If the team keeps student success at the center of the transformation process, the change will be efficient and sustainable. Before beginning the transformation process, school leaders must lead the process of creating a school vision that is inspiring and focused on student success.

The vision's journey, the journey to becoming the best learning organization for students, will not occur overnight, but in fact, can take months or even years to achieve. No matter how long the transformation process takes, there must be a team of vision champions who are willing to be part of the journey and go the length of the journey. The number of phases that make up the journey is determined by the current state of the school and the school's vision.

As the school begins the journey, school leaders, teachers, and staff members must remember the importance of maintaining a laser focus on the school's vision, which requires that the school's team have a laser focus on student success. The success of students will always be unavoidable throughout the transformation process. Student success determines the school's success. Without student success, schools will not succeed.

School teams must have not only a laser focus on student success, but also on being Vision Champions. Vision Champions are school leaders, teachers, and staff members who, no matter the circumstance, strive to be the best; they persist in making sure that students are successful and are determined to continue the journey. Vision champions have a calling to create an inspiring learning experience and environment for students.

As a result, the army of Vision Champions must be ready to do whatever it takes to ensure student success; must stand ready to step up to the plate, to push the boundaries of learning so that all students will experience success. Vision Champions are prepared to help all students—regardless of whether the students are high performing or at-risk.

School leaders must continue to reiterate the understanding that for schools to succeed, students must achieve first. Vision Champions wholeheartedly not only believe student success is required, but also model being the champions of not only the school but also the students. The school's vision must challenge stakeholders to push the boundaries and help all students to succeed. This starts with ensuring that all students have access to supports and services—to address academic, mental, and physical needs.

When students feel that the school is meeting their needs and the school leaders, teachers, and staff are there to help them succeed, they view learning in positive terms. Though Vision Champions will not be with students at all times, the relationships and connections that they form help students to make it in class, in school, and at home. Students need to know that principals, teachers, and instructional aides have their backs and they are there to support them during the good and bad times.

Think of Vision Champions as the 12th Man, the fans who are in the stands at all home Texas A&M football games. The fans become an extra defensive player who has helped propel Texas A&M into one of the most dominant college football teams in the nation. Vision Champions are no different as school leaders, teachers, and staff look to create the best learning opportunities and experiences for students. Every word of encouragement, pat on the back, and push across the finish line becomes invaluable to students and the success of the school.

Vision Champions must also realize that each student brings with them to school, each day, a unique set of skills and talents. Every child in school has a story that needs to be told, and school teams must make sure that each student's voice is heard. Throughout the transformation process, it is important to tell your school's story but also to listen to students and other stakeholders. Schools that begin the transformation process should be excited to tell their story and have an unyielding eagerness to empower students to tell their story.

The change process is challenging; therefore, school leaders, teachers, staff members, and members of the greater school community should be proud of their accomplishments and not be afraid of setbacks. Vision Champions need to make sure that they are listening to students. School leaders, teachers, and staff members must make the time to listen to students, as they address their needs, adapt learning to their interests, and help them to achieve their goals. For students to experience success, learning must be relevant and the school must be student-friendly.

Vision Champions have an unyielding determination to make sure that students succeed. Schools today must raise their expectations. The expectation for students to be the best is growing with each passing day. Society expects schools to help students succeed. Schools must remove barriers that prevent students from succeeding. Student success begins with having an inspiring school vision. An inspiring school vision is the result of school leaders, teachers, and staff members believing in students and working with them as a team. Additionally, as a team, they ensure that the school vision is based on hope and inspiration.

Students need to be empowered and inspired to be great, to take risks, and to be creative. Vision Champions, no matter what, are cheerleaders. They cheer during the good times and cheer even louder during periods of struggle. Did you know that students will model the behaviors of the "top five people they spend the most time with?" All the more reason for school leaders, teachers, and staff members to be positive, inspiring, and motivating. Vision Champions (great leaders, educators, staff members) focus on the positives as students experience success.

Today, become a Vision Champion for students and remember that every student, every teacher and staff member, parent and community member is vision critical in your school's journey to becoming the best. Vision Champions do not stop pushing forward, striving to be the best for students and creating the best learning opportunities and experiences for students. Today, become the Vision Champion that will propel your students to the top.

Strategy: Realize The Time Is Now!

"Sometimes there is no next time, no time-outs, no second chances. Sometimes it's now or never."

—Alan Bennett

To be clear, now is the perfect time to create a long-term vision that will help transform the school into a student-centered organization. With so many changes occurring in education, there must be a sense of urgency in every school. The growing demands for students to succeed and schools to produce, school leaders, teachers, and staff members need a uniting vision encourages strategic change to take place quickly. The school's vision must set the expectation in regards to student success, instructional effectiveness, and transformation process.

A typical school leader can always kick the proverbial can down the road for someone else to address. A visionary leader grabs the bull by the horn and begins the transformation process as soon as he or she is named principal or when the opportunity presents itself. Visionary school leaders act to create and implement a uniting school vision that sets the course to ensure success through the transformation process. A visionary leader ignites a sense of urgency in others and a sense of enthusiasm among teachers, staff members, and other stakeholders to help transform the school.

Today is an incredibly important milestone in a school's transformative journey to become the best school for students. No matter the obstacle, the challenge, or setback, school leaders, teachers, and staff members must remain focused on student success. Each day presents an opportunity to push the boundaries, to think strategically to move students to the next level. Developing a strategic focus can help school teams to remain focused even during times of uncertainty and as challenges are presented.

It is imperative that schools today focus on creating a culture of innovation, collaboration, and risk-taking throughout the teaching and learning process. School transformation starts with a clear and measurable vision. The vision must be inspiring, challenging, and innovative. High-performing schools have vision statements that are simple and concise so that stakeholders can remember them easily.

Simplicity helps to encourage commitment by interested parties and the willingness to embrace higher expectations and the challenges that will be along the school's journey. Now is the time for school leaders, teachers, and staff members to push their capabilities and strive to reach even higher levels of success for students. As the school's vision is strategic, no one should remain stationary, but always challenge their abilities to ascend the highest mountain. As the school grows through the transformation process, the school's vision only becomes more embedded into the work and ingrained in the school's culture.

Now is the time to create opportunities to engage all students in the learning process by transforming the school's culture and structures. Though engagement of all students will require that processes or models of learning are changed, ultimately school leaders, teachers, and staff members must push the boundaries so that the academic needs and interests of students are met. The transformation process will not be easy, but that is not to say we should not be pushing students to reach higher expectations.

In fact, our expectations for all students must always be at the highest level possible. The only change is that we must provide students with the resources and supports necessary to help them climb the ladder to success. Success is possible through effective implementation of a laser focus on student success and usage of strategic strategies. With mounting competition and increasing expectations, more so than in the past, now is the time that schools focus relentlessly on student success.

A strategic focus on student success together with a clear and concise school vision on student success will help propel the school to the top. As schools begin the transformation process and develop a student-centered vision, they should keep in mind what Frank Lloyd Wright—the famous American Architect—said: "I know the price of success: Dedication, Hard Work, and an unremitting devotion to the things you want to see happen."

Schools have the best opportunity to change and become student-centered. Many schools today are doing a fantastic job of preparing students. Though improvements have been made, now is the time to continue to push the boundaries and meet the needs of even more students. School leaders, teachers, and staff members have the best jobs in the world—embrace the chance to do something great for students by embracing the transformation process. School teams must work together to develop a clear and concise school vision that challenges the status quo and pushes learning and achievement levels to new heights.

Strategy: Create Centers of Inspiration

"It is never too late to be what you might have been."

—T. S. Eliot

As students face increased pressures as a result of high-stakes testing, increasing global competition, and increasing personal struggles, the job of educators is to transform schools into centers of inspiration. Teachers share in the responsibility to create schools that are places that encourage students to dream and to be innovative. More importantly, schools must be places where students feel safe—as an increasing number of students are coming to schools to escape the verbal, physical, and sexual abuse they experience at home—if they have a home.

The vision for schools must be parallel with the needs of students, a place that can meet all of their personal and academic needs. To transform schools, we must move from Cold War models focused on educating students using single modes of instruction into new centers focused on personalized learning. Stakeholder collaboration will be critical, starting with a team-developed vision for the school.

As schools begin to revise their vision and begin the transformation process, it will be important that students are inspired to push the boundaries of their learning. School leaders must lead the visioning process, encouraging teachers to be student-centered and creating a school filled with classrooms that inspire students to dream and be innovative. As schools seek to transform and become places where students are inspired to dream, school leaders, teachers, and staff members will need to become facilitators of learning, as well as cheerleaders for students as they take risks in their learning process.

Having an inspiring school vision requires classrooms and schools to be flexible, meeting the needs of all students and challenging them, while encouraging students to be innovative and take risks, while removing the fear of failure. For schools to become centers of inspiration, having a vision that encourages students to dream, schools must become less rigid throughout the teaching and learning process.

Supporting more flexible structures and systems will help meet the needs of all students, while also challenging them to meet new, higher expectations. Schools today—which is why having a transformative vision is necessary—must have engaging classrooms that inspire students to be innovative. Less rigid teaching and learning will also empower students to be "leaders of their learning" daring to be great without fear of failure.

Empowering students, along with stakeholders, to be leaders is quite simply a fundamental principle of a school's transformative journey. Schools with a clear and concise vision have an excellent opportunity to do something amazing for students, if school leaders, teachers, and staff members embrace the challenge and dare to push their own limits and leave their own zones of comfort.

As we know, as students are inspired, their attendance and achievement increase. Now is the time for schools to embrace this opportunity to push the boundaries and create learning that is challenging, relevant, engaging, but above all else, inspiring. The vision for school transformation must encourage school leaders, teachers, and staff members to let go and think outside the box.

According to Nelson Mandela, "It always seems impossible until it's done." Transformation is hard and may seem impossible; however, school officials and staff members must have the same growth mindset as Mandela encourages. School staffs push themselves and tackle what they may perceive as impossible so that they model the determination and tenacity to never give up for students. If leaders and teachers focus on the possibilities that the transformation can offer schools, and not on the obstacles, students will be inspired and reach new, higher levels of success.

The goal is to transform schools into centers of inspiration. School leaders, teachers, and staff members must coach students on how to aspire to be the best. There are no limits that schools can reach if creativity and innovation are at the center of their vision. Educators must continue to challenge the status quo and focus on creating schools that are characterized by innovation, inspiration, and creativity. To achieve these transformative benchmarks, all stakeholders must embrace collaboration, where everyone, including students, is at the decision-making table. Empowering student voices only leads to greater student engagement and success.

As the school reaches each milestone along the transformative journey, it must seek to reach higher levels of student success and become even more student-centered. Transformation requires that schools establish clear and attainable goals each year. Though many may doubt the school's ability to reach higher levels of success and become more student-centered, the determination to become centers of inspiration must guide the school's commitment to succeed for students. Schools must be the beacon of hope and inspiration for students. By transforming into learning organizations that have student success at the core of the vision, they become the pinnacle of success for others to follow.

Schools can change and become places that ignite levels of inspiration in students that will help propel them to success. Schools must seek to reach higher levels, a higher mountain peak. In simple terms, by embracing the challenge to turn the impossible into the possible, we help students to become great. Schools must never settle for average or low achievement levels; instead, they must strive to attain the highest achievement levels possible so that students succeed and are prepared for the next level.

Strategy: Develop a Focused Vision

"Where there is no vision, there is no hope."

—George Washington Carver

As schools reach each milestone along the transformative journey, school leaders, teachers, and staff members must keep focused and utilize every opportunity to help students experience success. Big things for students do not happen when educators only exert half their effort; when educators use their full effort and focus on what matters the most, students succeed.

By creating a school vision that is always about student success, schools ensure that learning programs are relevant and prepare students to be competitive on the world stage. Alexander Graham Bell said, "Concentrate all of your thoughts on the work at hand. The sun's ray does not burn until brought to a focus." A school will only succeed when student success is at the core of the vision and their work.

For students to be successful in today's schools, school leaders, teachers, and staff members must be willing to make learning relevant and engaging. Students today expect that schools provide the best learning opportunities possible that are relevant, innovative, and engaging. By creating a school vision that encourages risk-taking without the fear of failure, teachers are empowered to push the limits of the learning process.

The vision must also help school leaders, teachers, and staff members go the extra mile for students each day and do great things for students every day. School administrators, teachers, and staff members must have the same focus that Bell speaks about—a strategic direction that ignites learning and results in student success. When the rays of the sun are focused, energy is created.

When school leaders, teachers, and staff members focus on the success of all students, energy forms in the classroom, the school, and district. More importantly, students are energized to succeed. If students see the adults in their lives are committed to their success and willing to do whatever it takes to ensure their success, great things happen, as students are prepared to take risks and become leaders of their learning.

School leaders, teachers, and staff members must believe that they have the ability to do great things for students. Believing in their abilities as educators starts with a commitment to exert 100 percent of their energy to the school's vision—being the best school for all students. As the staff within the school begins to work diligently to ensure student success—the school's vision will continue to help the school remain focused on student success. The school's vision provides the cover for risk-taking and pushing the limits to ensure student success.

No matter the work in the school, the focus must remain the same, to ensure that all students experience success. As school leaders, teachers, and staff members focus on student success—the focused rays that develop will help move the success of all students to a higher level. Socrates says, "The secret of change is to focus all of your energy, not on fighting the old, but on building the new." Schools no longer have time to focus on yesterday's failures or defeats. To become schools that students need school leaders, teachers, and staff members must look to the future.

At the end of the day, the transformation process helps school leaders, teachers, and staff members discover their ability and power collectively to do something awesome for students. Utilizing the school's vision as the driving force behind change, school leaders can help the school transform. School leaders, teachers, and staff members must also realize that their efforts and commitment have an impact on student success—directly and indirectly.

When school teams fail to put forth their best efforts or fail to develop a transformative school vision, students will fail to succeed. Students want to be challenged, engaged, and empowered throughout the learning process. School staffs must create opportunities that require students to apply knowledge to real-world situations and encourage students to have an entrepreneurial and innovative spirit.

This type of learning requires personalization and willingness to push the limits by teachers. Likewise, a student must have a voice in new forms of learning—the ability to lead their learning and identify learning opportunities that are suited to their interests and goals. Students must be prepared to compete on a global stage, which requires new forms of teaching. Education must become more flexible and less rigid to move student success to the next level.

School leaders, teachers, and staff members must never lose sight of the school's vision. There must be a firm belief by all that they can move student success to the next level—by transforming the school's structures, processes, and systems. When effective, the transformation process seeps into all of the facets of the teaching and learning process. By relying on the school's vision as the blueprint for student-centered transformation, school leaders, teachers, and staff members can push the limits of success and make lasting change for the school.

Schools must embrace the continuous improvement process—as school leaders, teachers, and staff members embrace change or shifts in thinking. Schools today must focus on student success by creating the best learning experiences for students. As students succeed, school leaders, teachers, and staff members succeed. Today's educators must be driven by the unshakable faith that they can help all students succeed if their focus is in the right place.

Strategy: Focus on Engagement and Vision

> "If you want an engaged workforce, pay attention to how you create a vision, link people's work to your company's larger purpose."

> —Annie McKee

Many school leaders often forget a key stakeholder in the educational process. Many school leaders always talk about students, parents/guardians, community members, and business partners. They realize that without these critical stakeholder groups, the educational process proves to be difficult. But notice the stakeholder group that is often forgotten as schools look to create a culture of engagement: educators.

For the purpose of this book, the term "educators" includes school administrators, bookkeepers, custodians, and bus drivers—all school employees. As repeatedly mentioned throughout this book, all school staff shares the burden of educating students; therefore, they must all be engaged in the learning process. If students are not engaged, we need to figure out why and develop strategies that will lead to increased student engagement.

Engagement of stakeholders in the transformation is essential to the success of the change process. Think of participation of all stakeholders in the transformation process as vision critical. Vision critical begins by educators being engaged in the process. If schools expect students to be engaged in the classroom, then the school, school leaders, teachers, and staff must first be involved in the educational process. Too often, too many staff members remain on the sidelines—being comfortable with others performing the work. Transformation requires all staff members to be engaged—as the work is complex, high-energy, and fast-paced.

The school's transformation process requires the engagement of school leaders, teachers and staff members in developing the blueprint for change. Likewise, the school vision must be created through the same level of collaboration. As stakeholders assist in creating the vision and plan for transformation, they are more willing to be engaged and part of the process. Neither transformation nor vision development can be isolated to just a few if the goal is to create lasting change. Furthermore, change is improved through the engagement and empowerment of diverse perspectives.

The possibilities of student success exponentially increase when everyone is engaged and committed to their success. Educators must model the expectation to always look for ways to improve so that students never stop learning and pursuing greatness. Furthermore, educators must realize greatness isn't a given or a final destination, but is always moving, challenging them to meet new levels of greatness so that students experience success.

A collaboratively, well-developed school vision requires that school leaders, teachers, and staff members be champions for students. To be champions for students, educators must actively engage in the educational process and work to remove barriers that prevent students from succeeding. By working together, educators can help students overcome the most challenging obstacles. The school's vision challenges educators to meet students where they are and build relationships and connections with them that will help them overcome obstacles and to push through barriers that prevent them from success.

When educators work collaboratively and become champions for students, student success will skyrocket. Never underestimate the power of connections and hope as it pertains to student success. When students trust their teachers and have hope, great things happen academically for them. All students need a champion, that one adult who is there no matter the circumstance or situation. A transformative school vision requires this level of student attention by all staff members.

Be engaged in the educational process. There are several opportunities where all stakeholders, including educators, can be active leaders in the school. If opportunities don't exist, create them. The goals and expectations for the school are extremely high as the transformation process begins. School leaders, teachers, and staff members must all be engaged in the learning process, as the transformation process begins and the school's focus shifts to student success.

Strategy: Be a Beacon of Light

"We are told to let our light shine, and if it does, we won't need to tell anybody it does. Lighthouses don't fire cannons to call attention to their shining—they just shine a light."

—Dwight L. Moody

As the urgency grows to transform schools into learning institutions that are student-centered, school leaders must continue to communicate the need to remain focused on the importance of student success. School leaders, teachers, and staff members are reminded that "maybe they are the lighthouse in someone's storm." The goal of transformation is to create schools that adapt to meet the changing needs of students by becoming more personable.

For far too long, schools have been too rigid, operating as if all students needed the same supports and had the same interests. The rigidity found throughout the educational process is the very reason why schools must transform. The school's vision is the beacon that guides the way for day-to-day operations, teaching, and learning, as well as the transformation process.

Each day, school leaders, teachers, and staff members work hard to ensure students experience success, but as times change and the demographics of students continue to diversify, schools must become more adaptable to change—more quickly. The needs of students change almost on a daily basis—as students transfer from school to school as parents move to find jobs or become homeless. The changes among the student population are real and felt in every school. No school is isolated from change; therefore, schools must be willing and able to change.

Developing a uniting school vision that is inspiring and transformative will not be an easy process, nor will it occur overnight. All great things are the result of hard work and dedication from the individuals involved. If school visions are created for the right purpose, to help the school to focus on students, the vision becomes the beacon to all stakeholders.

The school's purpose unites people behind the focus and contributes to transforming the school's culture to meet the needs of students. The level of commitment of stakeholders to the school's vision is a good indicator of student success. Obviously, if the commitment is small, student success will be low; however, if stakeholders have bought into the school's vision, student success will he high.

Just as lighthouses guide ships safely into port, the school's vision will help transform the school. By using the school's vision to guide the transformation process, school leaders, teachers, and staff members become beacons of creativity, confidence, inspiration, and hope to students. When the school's vision has a laser focus on student success, teams are more willing to adopt the motto "do whatever it takes" so that students are successful. Just by having a positive, growth mindset, students notice the school's commitment to their success and will become more engaged in learning (which results in higher student success).

School leaders, teachers, and staff members today must be the beacon of hope for students. They must always keep in mind that many of today's students are coming to school with health, home, or learning issues. Furthermore, more and more students have self-esteem issues—doubting their abilities to succeed. As such, each day, school leaders, teachers, and staff members must be the beacon of hope and provide words of hope and inspiration, sheltering students from fear and offering encouragement during times of struggle.

Schools that are student-focused, high-energy, and charismatic are the result of having a clear, concise school vision that creates the expectation for school leaders, teachers, and staff members to push the limits and do whatever it takes to help students succeed and be college-, career-, and life-ready.

There are so many things that confront and challenge today's youth. Each day, the battle undoubtedly sends students' anxiety levels through the roof, as they question their abilities to succeed or lack the self-confidence to persevere through obstacles. It is the school's vision that helps to encourage school leaders, teachers, and staff members to be the beacon of light in the abyss for students. No matter the struggle, like Randi G. Fine said, "we must be the beacon of light in someone's darkness."

As schools transform, the expectation for all school leaders, teachers, and staff members to step forward to help all students to overcome challenges becomes ingrained in the school's culture. The more schools are willing to focus on addressing the individual needs and goals of students, the more students will succeed. Katrina Loukas said, "Be that beacon. Let your light radiate—no more apologizing for your light quotient!"

School leaders, teachers, and staff members will never reach a quota when it comes to being the light for students. Students will always need help, need school leaders, teachers, and staff members who are willing to go the extra mile to ensure their success and offer words of hope in times of darkness. Transformed schools communicate hope, not fear and desperation. Transformed schools inspire imagination and creativity that results in increased student engagement and achievement! Does your school do these things?

TRANSFORMATIVE IDEAS FROM THE FIELD

The principalship with each passing school year is becoming more difficult. School principals are not only expected to be instructional leaders, but also managers of day-to-day operations, the public relations officer for the school, counselor, and so many other things to so many. By creating a school vision that empowers others to be leaders and change agents, the complexities that schools face can be better addressed by school principals.

Removing barriers to success, in other words, reducing the complexities in schools, begins with the school leader communicating the need for a school vision that encourages change. School principals cannot lead the transformation process alone, nor can they create a school vision alone. Transformative school principals create opportunities where all stakeholders have a voice in the development of the vision and creating the blueprint for change.

It is important for school principals to seek out diverse perspectives as they lead vision development. The more voices a school principal can capture through feedback and input, the more unifying the vision will be. We recommend that school principals start with a simple, inspiring school vision that can be understood by all so that the transformation is not derailed. Transformation is a challenging process; school principals do not need to add additional complexities to the process, which is why the vision for the school needs to remain simple and concise.

PRINCIPAL'S NOTE

"Leadership is the ability to turn vision into reality."
—Warren Bennis

9 a.m.
August 22
Welcome back staff meeting
Spring Water Elementary School Library

I was excited to take on the role as principal of Spring Water Elementary School. I had just finished up five years as a middle school principal at a turnaround school and was looking for a new challenge. Even with five years under my belt as a school administrator, I was still nervous about meeting the staff, getting to know their personalities, understanding the parent culture, and working with a new set of students.

I was eager to get my hands dirty and dive into this new adventure. I was also excited to put down some roots. My previous assignment was at a school thirty-five miles from my house. I was glad to be closer to home. I was ready to put down some roots and stick it out for the long haul. I was all set for my first official day at my new school.

The staff was a mix of ages, experiences, and backgrounds. There were teachers with doctorate degrees in education and master's degrees in early literacy. A few of the teachers had over forty years of teaching experience. Many of them had been teachers for fifteen to twenty years. In a strange twist of fate, I was the youngest staff member. I was also their leader.

I opened my staff meeting with your standard set of icebreakers (marshmallow tower building, two truths and a lie, etc.) I talked a little about myself, my family, and my experiences in education. I wanted them to get to know me and I wanted to get to know them. Then, I asked the staff to share out what made our school special and different from other schools so that I could get a sense of what made the school tick. In another sense, if the district needed to close schools due to budgetary concerns, why should our school stay open?

No response.

I thought that maybe my question was too broad. So asked them to think about getting into an elevator with someone. If they had to describe the school that they worked at to that person before they got to their floor, could they do it? This was a strategy that my dissertation chair had given to me a few years back. If you can give a stranger a clear picture of where your organization is at that moment and where it is headed in a short amount of time, then you have a strong grasp of the vision of your organization.

I got crickets.

"What gets you excited about teaching?"

Virtual tumbleweeds rolled across the room.

"Are there any exciting new initiatives you would like to engage in?" More silence.

Finally, I got a response. "We assign a lot of homework," said one teacher.

"We are stricter than other schools," said another.

These were not the responses I was anticipating.

It was then that I realized why I had been hired to be the principal at Spring Water Elementary School. The school lacked vision. Don't get me wrong. The teaching staff at this school was amazing. They were all hard working, dedicated, and had high expectations for their students. They were skilled instructors and the test scores at the school were second to none.

However, the status quo from twenty years ago was still considered best practice. As a whole, teachers got up every morning, drove to school, closed the classroom door behind them, and engaged with children in the same way that they had done for decades. As the meeting progressed, I heard a phrase that strikes fear into the heart of any leader when learning about an organization and when asking about the reasons for certain procedures and practices.

"This is the way we have always done it." Rear Admiral Grace Hopper wrote that this is the most dangerous phrase in our language. She was right. This line of thinking doesn't allow for new ideas, new directions, or innovation. It was time to transform this school. It was time to bring stakeholders together to create a vision for the school that was inspiring, purposeful, and forward-thinking.

It was vital that I connect with all stakeholders to ensure that all viewpoints were out in the open. These stakeholder groups included teachers, parents, students, and community leaders. Together, we would create a vision that would be in the best interest of the children we are serving. I met with different stakeholder groups over the next few weeks. It was interesting to learn that some groups wanted sweeping changes made to the school.

These changes included relaxing strict rules, more student-centered programs around social emotional learning, and an increase in educational technology. Other groups wanted to hold onto decades-old traditions and customs. I knew that in order to be a successful leader, I must take all of these considerations into account, as well as my own passions, which were centered around inclusion, intervention, and innovation.

All of these different elements defined our school. However, we needed to define how they fit together to create our identity as a school. It was time to get packing.

We were about to go on a journey.

TAKEAWAY IDEAS

- The school's vision is the roadmap that will lead to transformation.
- Transformation is a process that will help the school fulfill its core principles outlined in the school's vision.
- Schools go through the transformation process to increase student success, by establishing effective leadership structures and implementing a more personalized approach to learning.
- Involving stakeholders in the creation of the school's vision and setting the goals for transformation will help lead to better outcomes for the school and students.
- A clear and concise vision statement will lead to increased commitment and buy-in from stakeholders.
- School transformation must start with a clear purpose that is established by the school's vision.

Chapter Two

Journey

Preparing for an Epic Blastoff

Journey

The time for change is now. There is a growing urgency for schools to transform into organizations that are more personalized and adaptable to the changing and diverse needs of students. However, as Beyersdorf indicates, though schools may need to change quickly, quality must not be sacrificed. School transformation requires a strategy to develop the systems that will lead to an effective teaching and learning process, environment, and organization. All of which takes time.

To those school leaders who are thinking about beginning the transformation process, slow down and develop a strategic plan that outlines the measurable goals for students, teachers, staff members, and the school. For those school leaders who are already in the middle of the transformation process, you still have time to slow the process down to ensure that the change process is leading to the desired results. In too many schools, quality is often sacrificed for speed, which ultimately leads to other issues further into the journey—specifically capacity to lead change and the sustainability of the transformation efforts.

TRANSFORMATIVE CORE IDEA

School transformation is a journey, not a destination. In other words, school transformation is an ongoing process that will need to be continuously modified to remain aligned to the changing needs of the school, students, and teachers.

All great journeys begin with making a decision—to take the first step. School transformation is indeed a journey that will require a team effort. The needs, goals, and aspirations of students will without question change throughout the process. School leaders will need to help stakeholders understand that the transformation process will be an ongoing process that will continually change to meet the needs of students. As destination signals an end, there is no finish line for the transformation process.

TRANSFORMATIVE KEY UNDERSTANDINGS

* *Inclusive*—the change process is inclusive—embracing the diversity of stakeholders. Schools that include all stakeholders in the transformation process have stronger results as stakeholders are empowered to be leaders and part of the decision-making process.
* *Endurance*—the journey leads to a more focused and effective leadership process, teaching process, and learning process. The journey helps school leaders to develop the tenacity to work through current and future challenges.
* *Uniqueness*—the change process leads to creating a unique, innovative, and personalized teaching and learning program for students.
* *Teamwork*—the journey unites stakeholders and grows a culture of collaboration.
* *Growth of Staff*—the journey is focused on improving student success by enhancing the effectiveness of leaders, teachers, and staff members.
* *Extraordinary*—teachers and staff members are encouraged to do extraordinary things for students.

TRANSFORMATIVE ROLES

School Leaders:

* Lead the transformation process;
* Communicate and share progress made;
* Assist stakeholders to overcome obstacles, setbacks, and barriers;
* Focus stakeholders on the transformation goals and vision.
* Evaluate progress regularly.

Teachers and Staff Members:

- Actively engage in the transformation process;
- Focus on the success and preparedness for the next level of students;
- Engage in professional learning;
- Are willing to take risks and push boundaries.

RESEARCH AND TRANSFORMATION

The word "journey" is not mentioned in the research regarding organizational transformation. However, the term "journey" is found in books and articles about personal and spiritual transformation. This is both validating and interesting. Transformation is more than just changing school structures. If done effectively, transformation also changes school leaders, teachers, and staff members' professional practice.

As mentioned in the first principle, vision, transformation must result in changes for students. As such, even in school transformation, which is a form of organizational transformation, transformation is a personal and organizational process. Furthermore, researchers contend that the journey is spiritual or at least inspirational. As school leaders, teachers, and staff members, what are you, as a team, creating for students?

If that isn't inspiring, then you need to perform a self-check about why you want to begin the transformation process, and more importantly, why you want to be a school leader, teacher, or staff member. The journey or the process will be difficult. According to Hoyte and Greenwood (2007), the journey will face several obstacles, one being complacency. Additionally, Hoyte and Greenwood give credence to the fact that school leaders must continue to refocus stakeholders throughout the journey. Beginning the transformation process is not enough; maintaining a laser focus on purpose for change will be needed throughout the journey.

Early wins are significant; however, they will need to be put in the context of the larger goals of the transformation process. We encourage school leaders to use early wins as milestone markers along the overall journey. Benefiel (2005) goes a step further and explains that the school leader's ability to inspire stakeholders will be essential to overcoming obstacles that will surely appear throughout the organizational journey. She adds that schools that have a high "spiritual" culture will be more successful in remaining on course throughout the transformation process, but that culture is often a reflection of the school leader's belief.

The school leader has a lot of influence on not only beginning the transformation process, but also how the transformation plays out. The school's transformative journey can be a road filled with potholes or a yellow-brick road that is enjoyable and empowering to all and results in conditions that will lead to student success. We also recognize the need for school leaders to remain attentive to stakeholders' needs, attitudes, and change.

Tichy and Devanna (1987) reiterate the fact that the organization cannot change faster than the people involved. As such, school leaders must perform regular "pulse checks" along the transformative journey to ensure that stakeholders remain engaged and aligned with the transformation's vision. As the journey progresses along, the school leader's involvement must be based on the needs of the school and its people. Nevertheless, the school leaders will always need to, at the very least, be the cheerleader, coach, counselor. As the transformation's navigator, the school leader makes changes based on metrics, observations, and feedback.

TRANSFORMATIVE POINTS TO CONSIDER

- The transformation process is long; however, the results for students can be rewarding if the school principal leads by empowering others to be transformative leaders.
- The principalship is a journey that should be transformative from the start. School principals who realize how awesome the principalship can be are the same principals who transform schools.
- As the journey will have ups and downs, educators must always keep their focus on the students—it will make the challenges all the more worth it, even when the doubters become loud. Press forward, stay focused, and celebrate when students succeed!
- Challenges, obstacles, failure, and sweat are terms that come to mind when many school leaders, teachers, and staff members think of their experience of transformation. The journey may be long, but schools must transform in order to remain relevant.
- Allow transformation to be personal more than just changing school structures, but also life-changing to all those involved.

PRACTICAL INTRODUCTION

School leaders must understand that transformation is a journey, an ongoing change process. Often, transformation is seen in terms of a process with a beginning and ending; however, it is an ongoing process that challenges school leaders and stakeholders to continually seek opportunities to improve. Throughout the transformative journey, there will be several obstacles, setbacks, and barriers; school leaders must help stakeholders to continue to push forward.

All great journeys have a starting point. From the beginning, the transformation process must be strategic and focused on increasing student success. School leaders must be prepared to help keep the focus on the journey—ultimately the change process and strategic plan. The strategic plan can serve as an excellent roadmap for the transformation process when used effectively. As the transformation process is an ongoing journey, without a destination, a strategic plan can help to keep the focus on the school's long-term goals and the needs of students.

From the beginning, school leaders must communicate that change is a long-term process that will lead to improvements for students, teachers, staff, and the greater school community. Furthermore, school leaders must communicate and help others to understand that change takes time to occur; however, they (all stakeholders) must remain focused and committed to transforming the school. Though change takes time to become engrained in the school's DNA, there must always be a sense of urgency for students to experience success.

KEY QUESTIONS

The Key Questions are meant to help school leaders begin thinking about the transformation principles in relation to their schools.

- Identify the actual/possible challenges that will hinder the school's transformation.
- Discuss the systems that are currently in place that will help the transformation to continue when confronted with challenges, obstacles, or setbacks.
- What is the role of the school's principal, teachers, and staff when setbacks occur?
- How can challenges help strengthen the school's transformation process?
- How will the school's plan for transformation lead to improved professional practice?

JOURNEY TRANSFORMED

Though the journey to transform may go by quickly, it is important not to rush the process. Each day the countdown clock continues to move quickly to zero. School leaders must work to keep everyone's attention on the purpose of the transformation and keep reminding everyone that transformation is a marathon, not a race. Though urgency to change may exist, having a strategic

pace to allow for capacity to grow will aid the school later in the transformation process.

Furthermore, the most important thing to keep in mind throughout the
transformative journey is monitoring student achievement. Student achievement is the way schools begin the transformation process. Typically low
student achievement sends the signal there are organizational, cultural,
leadership or, instructional issues that must be changed. Educators often try
to boil the ocean—taking a scattered approach to creating change. If school
leaders take a more strategic approach to the transformation process, then the
result will be more buy-in, sustainability, and student success. As the school
begins the transformative journey, collaboration will be key to the overall
success of the change that occurs within the school.

Transformation cannot be done in silos, but out in the open, where school
leaders, teachers, and staff members can work together to create lasting change.
To be effective—that is, to really increase student learning and create a school
culture that is student-centered—the journey must be collaborative. Furthermore, systems and protocols that have the success of students at the core will
prove to be invaluable throughout the school's transformative journey.

Strategy: Brace Yourself!

"All journeys have secret destinations of which the traveler is unaware."

—Martin Buber

The journey is about to begin and be prepared for amazing things to happen as
the school focuses on student achievement and creating a culture that is transformative. To maximize the journey's potential, school leaders, teachers, and
school staff will need to be willing to venture outside of their comfort zones,
challenge the status quo, and take risks. At the end of the day, educators must
do what they believe is necessary to help all students succeed.

Educators must not be afraid to be innovative throughout the journey, think
outside the box, or flip the script in order to engage students and make learning relevant to students' interests. Our charge is to always push the envelope
in order to meet the needs of all students. School leaders, teachers, and staff
members must pace themselves, understanding when to speed up and slow
down based on the needs of the school and students.

As the journey begins to result in changes in the school and students begin
to succeed, a winning, student-centered culture begins to take root. As the
school begins to climb higher and reach higher levels of success, educators
must remain focused on the success of the individual student and ensure
that protocols remain in place that will help to sustain success. Keep in
mind that one student can move the need higher or lower—so never forget

that the transformation process is always about ensuring the success of the individual student.

Understanding that transformation means better opportunities for students and having a laser focus on student success must be constantly at the forefront as the school makes strategic plans in the classroom and throughout the school. For the transformation journey to reap fruits of success for students, educators must push themselves to develop a stronger focus on student success. They must be willing to push the boundaries of the teaching and learning process, removing obstacles that are designed to derail the journey.

Students will succeed if educators are there to assist them during times of struggle and success. Developing a school culture that is based on shared decision-making and collaboration will help to ensure that students are successful throughout the change process. Though many see the transformative journey as being adult-driven, schools that empower students to also be change agents experience even greater results.

The key transformative point to keep in mind is to transform the teaching and learning process so that students experience success. In order to do this, schools must engage students more in identifying what needs to change. Instead of educators prescribing "remedies" to possible problems, students must be empowered to be change agents—and provide input throughout the transformative journey.

Strategy: Map the Importance of a Journey

"Sometimes it's the journey that teaches you a lot about your destination."

—Drake

Your school is about to embark on what will be a remarkable journey. As the school continues to move forward and grow, thanks to transformation, the journey continues—the success of all students remains the focus. Transformation challenges schools to change and become more adaptable to the needs and interests of students. Additionally, schools go through a change to create structures that will ensure the sustainability of systems and protocols that will result in long-term student success.

Success throughout the journey requires that school leaders, teachers, and staff members focus on creating an inspiring path for students that will lead to their success. Jeff Weiner, CEO of LinkedIn, a professional social media giant, suggests that many organizations are not inspirational:

The important word there is inspire. The key difference between managers and leaders is that managers tell people what to do, while leaders inspire them to do it. Inspiration comes from three things: clarity of one's vision, courage of their conviction and the ability to effectively communicate both of those things.

School leaders must work to make every opportunity for others to be part of the journey. They must communicate and model the desire that they want everyone to be part of the voyage and inspire them to be actively engaged in the mission. To be actively involved, school leaders must encourage stakeholders to utilize their skills and share their talents and ideas to make the transformation even more rewarding for the school, staff, and students.

Diverse perspectives result in stronger and more positive outcomes for students. Though the school's vision is focused solely on creating the best outcomes for students, the transformative journey will also result in better outcomes for all stakeholders. The school's vision results in better outcomes for all stakeholders by focusing on creating better lines of communication, a more positive culture in the organization and a shared, collective vision, purpose, and direction.

Instead of focusing on fear and desperation, school leaders, teachers, and staff members must focus on hope and inspiration. Hope and inspiration encourage stakeholders to be part of the journey, as the opposite turns stakeholders off. Starting the journey to transformation may seem overwhelming. To be clear, change is by no means small; instead, it is a lofty goal that will push the skills and abilities of the school.

As mentioned earlier, as the transformation process is challenging; all stakeholders must be working toward the same goal and operating using the same vision. School leaders must communicate that they want and expect stakeholders to be part of the journey. If for some reason they find that some stakeholders are reluctant to be part of the voyage, school leaders must extend the olive branch even further and be willing to make the extra effort to find ways to engage those reluctant few in the process.

Transformation requires a sense of team, based on trust and positive relationships. The transformative journey succeeds only with a team approach. Though many schools will tackle school transformation to focus on improving student achievement, other factors must be targeted that directly affect the success of students. Changing multiple components is all the more reason to look at school transformation as a journey—as it takes several "spokes to make a wheel strong enough to roll."

Change must address culture, systems, protocols, and policies. More importantly, school transformation creates the expectation that school leaders, teachers, and staff members bring their "A" game every day. They must realize that to be the best and create the best learning opportunities for students, they must also have this level of commitment to the journey. Embrace the journey that your school is beginning and watch what happens!

Strategy: Embrace the Mountain

"Every mountain top is within reach if you just keep climbing."

—Barry Finlay

The transformative journey requires (1) a laser focus on student success; (2) collaboration; (3) personal determination; (4) stakeholder leadership and empowerment; and (5) a fearless attitude. As the journey to transform the school begins, school leaders, teachers, and staff members must never settle for the bare minimum, only the best. Being average is never good enough when it comes to student success and creating the best learning opportunities for students.

As the transformation journey continues, school leaders, teachers, and staff members must not fear the mountains in the distance or that currently confront them. In fact, they must scale the highest mountains if they expect to reach the pinnacle of success. The higher the mountain, the bigger the challenge, the greater the opportunity, the bigger the reward. Transformative journeys that will take the school to the top require that school leaders, teachers, and staff members tackle the following: (1) personalized learning for all students; (2) collaboration; (3) risk-taking and innovation; (4) student voice; (5) teachers being lead learners; and (6) structures and systems that impede.

At the end of the day, school teams scale mountains by focusing on the success of the individual student. As a school, school leaders, teachers, and staff members must continue to look for ways to make learning more personalized. Classroom instructional strategies that target the whole class are quickly becoming obsolete and ineffective. As educators, they must view learning at the individual level and create systems that meet students where they are and push them to a higher standard of success based on personalized academic goals.

New forms of learning completely go against conventional wisdom and even age-old beliefs, but as the school begins the transformation process and ascends the tallest mountain, student success must be at the core of the journey. Even as obstacles appear, the success of students must be the fuel to help school teams push forward. The transformation process will undoubtedly be a challenge for many, but schools must transform and be better suited to meet the needs of an increasingly diverse student population.

The journey will be challenging to many teachers, especially as the teaching and learning process goes through changes. Students today expect to have collaborative, personalized, and performance-based learning opportunities, not just for a few classes, but in all of their classes. New forms of learning will be a huge mountain for many teachers to climb. Teachers must begin to view collaboration without walls, moving away from desks and walls and into open spaces that allow for movement and flexible learning environments.

As schools begin the transformation process, school leaders must help teachers and staff members look for new ways to offer students learning that is personalized and relevant to their goals. They must not be afraid to leave their classrooms, schools, or offices to collaborate with others. The mountains most feared by many are risk-taking and innovation. Educators fear change too much, which hinders student success. We must not fear the mountain of risk-taking. If we fail, we must fail fast and move on. Failure provides critical learning experiences that will move student success higher, if embraced.

Failure provides great learning experiences that can be used to create student-centered instructional programs. Critics who appear throughout the risk-taking process will be silenced by the sheer determination of transformative leaders, teachers, and staff members. The success of climbing the mountain will far outweigh those who bathe in doubt and use a towel that is stitched in desperation. Greatness does not occur without a spirit of innovation, risk-taking, and outside of the box thinking. The status quo is the enemy of greatness and success. We must stretch ourselves to reach the highest pinnacle.

Throughout the school transformation, student voice must be a point of focus. If educators listen closely, they have so much to offer that can help teachers to meet their needs and help them to accomplish their goals. Educators must come to grips with the fact that they rarely know everything and they must stop prescribing remedies without garnering input from their students. Educators must create opportunities that allow student voice to guide the direction of the journey as often as possible. Ultimately, the transformative journey is tied directly to student success.

Without student success, educators fail and ascension up the mountain stops short. To remove the possibility of failure, school leaders, teachers, and education leaders must engage and empower students to help develop the roadmap to transform the school. Schools do not fail by giving students a voice, only by limiting their voice. If school leaders, teachers, and staff members listen (no matter how uncomfortable it may be for them) to student input and feedback, they can climb any mountain that confronts them. A mountain that is often overlooked along the transformative journey is empowering teachers to be lead learners.

No mountain terrain is similar, as many rock climbers will attest. Neither is the transformation process, as each school experiences different transformations. They approach each mountain differently and take the time to study and learn the uniqueness of each mountain they choose to scale. Teachers, along with administrators, must model learning, which includes modifying instruction, processes, and systems to meet the needs of a diverse student body.

Teachers must be empowered to make the changes necessary to meet the needs of all students. Administrators must work to remove barriers and obstacles that prevent teachers from being leaders in the school. More importantly, school administrators must model embracing challenges as opportunities to grow. Additionally, highly effective school leaders embrace obstacles as a means to help the school move forward and help students to achieve greatness.

Embracing the mountain, the transformative journey, requires an innovative and determined spirit by all. A great quote by Trinity Bourne is, "The ones who climb the mountain don't wait for permission. They just start walking and climbing." No one needs permission to climb the mountain, to collaborate, to empower others, to be innovative—just do it. Sometimes asking permission is an obstacle in disguise that impedes or prevents change from occurring in schools.

Be not afraid to push the boundaries for students. Climb the mountain; better yet, form a team that will move student success to an even higher mountain peak. If you fail, fail fast and pick yourself up again; continue to ascend the mountain. Always seek higher mountains to climb so that more students will experience success. Positive, student-centered results are limitless.

Strategy: Understand that Testing Is Now in Progress

"Only those who will risk going too far can possibly find out how far one can go."

—T. S. Eliot

As schools begin the journey to transform, school leaders, teachers, and staff members will face several tests. The tests that confront them will challenge them to become better. Public educators hear this all the time: competition will help public education improve. Students today are looking for opportunities to access the best learning programs possible. Public school competition from private, charter, and home schools are challenging educators to stretch the boundaries of their abilities to continue to provide the best learning opportunities for students.

All great journeys face challenges along the way that are designed to test the adventurers' resiliency. As competition tests public educators' ability and willingness to succeed, the need for transformation will become more urgent. Public education must be more than just worksheets and assessments. Instead, public schools must be centers of learning and inspiration that encourage students to dream by challenging each student academically through real-world and rigorous experiences. The goal of the transformation process is creating learning programs that will prepare students for the global stage.

Educators today have an opportunity to change the dynamics of learning, but only if change is embraced. Many schools today are changing and implementing systems of personalized learning. With each passing day, many teachers are pushing the boundaries of the learning process so that students are provided the best opportunities to succeed. Several teachers are rock stars who understand that the test that educators face today is a chance to become better for students.

All of their actions speak to the quote by an anonymous author, "Walls aren't put in our lives to stop us, they are there to test how much we want something." School leaders, teachers, and staff members must have a laser focus on student success each mile along the transformative journey. A barrage of tests confronts schools each day. Think about the many tests that school leaders, teachers, and staff members must be prepared to handle, address, and help others to cope with each day before teaching can even begin.

Students, as a whole, are coming to school each day with various goals, needs (academic, mental, health, and social), and other challenges. As such, school teams must be prepared to step up and make sure that students are receiving the supports and services that they need to be successful. However, unlike in years past, schools today are being challenged, tested if you will, to drill down to the individual student. Schools must be able to transform systems so that the individual needs of all students are met.

The ability to meet the needs of individual students will be the catalyst that will help propel public schools into the future. To address the needs of individual students, personalized learning will need to be considered. In fact, personalized learning is a major test that many educators continue to struggle with and have not yet experienced. Teachers today must continue to focus on finding ways to meet the needs of each student, delivering just-in-time supports that help students to move, grow, and to be successful.

As school leaders, teachers, and staff members look to push the boundaries of the learning process throughout the transformative journey, student success will begin to increase. As schools transform into centers of inspiration and personalized learning, cookie-cutter approaches to learning will fade away. Remember that the most dangerous phrase in education is "we've always done it this way."

When educators fail to realize the need to change, students suffer. When schools become complacent and deaf to students' voices, students choose other means of education: the competition. School leaders, teachers, and staff members must always look for opportunities to grow and to become better for students. Just as the journey seems to be smooth, new tests will appear. Unlike other tests, the test that is confronting schools will only increase.

Public school competition will only increase, which is why schools need to begin to transform now. The public demands and expectations for public education will only continue to grow. A Chinese proverb says, "To get through the hardest journey, we need to take only one step at a time, but we must keep stepping." Though the pressures of educators may sometimes be overwhelming, teachers must stay focused on ensuring students succeed.

To perform well on this current test, teachers must continue to move forward. Within each challenge lies an opportunity to grow and become better for students. Transformation is exactly that opportunity for schools to meet the needs of students. With each step, educators develop the ability to confront the many challenges and competitions that face them today. The challenge and key is to keep stepping, moving forward, remaining focused on student success and not the noises that are designed to derail the school's journey.

Embrace every opportunity, no matter how big the challenge is, as overcoming problems help educators to become better for students. School leaders, teachers, and staff members must recognize opportunities for success even when tested. Even as schools succeed, there is always room to do a lot of work. By focusing on growth, having a growth mindset, educators can be prepared for any challenge that confronts them.

It would be wise to remember that Noah built the ark before the flood, not during the flood. Schools today prepare students for not only today's challenges, but also unknown problems in the future. Though schools face several tests today, what they do right now can help students to succeed. Vernon Law says, "Experience is the hardest kind of teacher. It gives you the test first and lesson afterward."

Educators must be proactive, instead of being reactive. Students today expect that classrooms be engaging, collaborative, and relevant. School leaders, teachers, and staff members can win if they recognize and embrace the need to change. Now is the time to listen to what students, parents/guardians, and the greater community is saying. By listening and accepting the challenge to create the best learning opportunities, experience, and environment, schools will be better prepared to face the tests the confront them along the transformative journey.

Remember, educators "do not have to see the whole staircase, just take the first step." Educators must continue to push the boundaries of the teaching and learning process along the journey. Educators must test themselves and challenge their abilities to meet the challenge. School leaders, teachers, and staff members must not be afraid to take risks if the goal is to increase student success.

Strategic risks throughout the transformative journey in pursuit of what is in the best interest of students must always be encouraged. Educators must face tests along the journey with fearless determination to succeed for students. Students will never reach the levels needed to be college-, career-, and life-ready if strategic risks are not taken. Ben Franklin once said, "I didn't fail the test. I just found one hundred ways to do it wrong."

As a team, school leaders, teachers, and staff members must have the same growth mindset as Franklin as they work together to transform the school. The test that currently stands in front of many schools is the challenge to create schools that are student-centered and with personalized modes of learning. As a team, schools pass the test and become better organizations for students, *if* they embrace the challenge and accept the need to change.

Though time is of the essence, change takes time and will not occur overnight. School leaders, teachers, and staff members must all take the first step and begin the transformative journey today. A quote from Beverly Sills speaks to how school leaders, teachers, and staff members must embrace the challenge: "You may be disappointed if you fail, but will be doomed if you don't try."

If schools fail to realize the opportunity that they have to transform structures, processes, and classrooms to be based solely on preparing students for success and readiness for the next level, then they fail students. Schools will never become the best if they are not willing to take risks and embrace change. Educators today will never be able to meet the changing needs of students if they never begin the journey to transform. Henry Ford once famously said, "Whether you think you can or think you can't, you're right." Educators must always exhibit confidence in their abilities to overcome tests so that students succeed.

Strategy: Understand DELTA

"And suddenly you know it's time to start something new and trust in the magic of beginnings."

—Mandy Hale

The journey to transforming today's schools is a remarkable process that will help strengthen schools' abilities to meet the needs of students. As schools begin the transformation journey, school leaders, teachers, and staff members must be Determined, Energized, Laser-focused, Targeted and All In! Be part of the DELTA force in your school that will help transform it.

First, school teams must all be *Determined* to ensuring that students succeed. No matter the obstacle, the struggle, or the setback, teams must be determined to work through the challenges to ensure students succeed. Remember that failure will never win if the determination to succeed is strong. School leaders must give the green light to teachers and staff members to push the boundaries of the learning process, to take risks and do whatever it takes to ensure students experience success. The transformative journey encourages school leaders to empower others as leaders.

By empowering others, schools are better positioned to beat the many challenges. As a team, school leaders, teachers, and staff members cannot let obstacles stand in their way to move students to the next level. Their determination for student success must be unyielding. Students today need educators to believe in their abilities, especially as the global competition continues to increase. The team's level of determination must reach the intensity that can propel any student to the next level.

Rocky, in the 2006 movie *Rocky Balboa*, said, "Every champion was once a contender that refused to give up." Educators, even as they experience challenges throughout the transformation process must believe that they can move students to have the confidence in their abilities as a team to succeed. For students to have a positive belief in themselves, school leaders, teachers, and staff members must believe in themselves.

Secondly, educators must be *Energized* about their roles and responsibilities. Throughout the transformation process, they must exhibit confidence, especially in front of students. Students are facing increasing pressures; as such they need self-confidence, and the more educators show confidence in themselves and their abilities, the more likely students will be confident in their abilities to tackle the pressures that they face. Confidence is contagious. Catch it and spread it. Understandably, as the transformation process continues, school leaders, teachers, and staff members become tired.

Nevertheless, they must realize that students need them to find the strength and energy to finish the journey strong and run across the finish line. Each day, educators should get a boost of energy when students enter the school. School leaders, teachers, and staff members are fortunate to have the best jobs in the world.

The more school leaders, teachers, and staff members are energized about what they do, the more students will be energized about attending school and learning. Schools and classrooms today must be places of high energy, positivity, and confidence as schools look to transform to meet the changing needs of students. It is in the best interest of school leaders, teachers, and staff members to ensure that students are confident and energized about their abilities. Educators must always be the ones in the room who are always confident, active, and excited to go the extra mile for students.

Third, as schools begin the transformation process, educators must have a *Laser focus* on student success. There is nothing more important in today's schools than student success. School leaders, teachers, and staff members must send a clear signal to all students that their success is their top priority. Bruce Lee, the martial arts movie star, said, "The successful warrior is the average man, with a laser-like focus." This quote speaks volumes as educators have the ability to help students experience success if they make the time to concentrate on the individual student.

Likewise, Michael Jordan challenges leaders to "focus like a laser, not like a flashlight." When educators have a laser focus on student success, nonrelevant noises are blocked out. Student success is the central component that is found throughout the transformation process. The whole basis for transformation must be to change the school and become student-centered, focused on doing whatever it takes to help students succeed!

Fourth, the teaching and learning process in today's schools must be *Targeted* to the academic needs of each student. Educators must drill down to the specific individual needs of students. Through the transformation process, focus on what each student needs so that he or she is successful. Here again it is important that school leaders, teachers, and staff members not to try and boil the ocean, but be strategic in their approach to ensuring student success.

In other words, focus specifically on what each student needs to be successful: transforming those systems, structures, and protocols that will lead to the greatest opportunities for student success. Mal Pancoast, a coach for school leaders, says, "The odds of hitting your target go up dramatically when you aim at the target." It does not take much to hit a goal, but the first step is always to identify the target.

As the transformative journey continues, school leaders, teachers, and staff members must be *All In!* School teams all have talents, skills, and experiences that can help students succeed. All team members must "do whatever it takes" and be willing to go the extra mile for students. Vince Lombardi, the legendary head coach the Green Bay Packers, said, "Most people fail, not because of lack of desire, but because of lack of commitment."

Being All In requires that school leaders, teachers, and staff members have a strategy with a strategic focus. Be not afraid to establish high expectations, take risks, and push the boundaries of the teaching and learning process as the school transforms. Abraham Lincoln said, "Commitment is what transforms promise into reality." As a school leader, you must be All In, committed to leading the transformation process of your school.

Embrace the transformative journey. Use the challenges as opportunities to push the boundaries of the teaching and learning process. Take the first step and begin the transformative process. Realize that change will only occur if the journey begins, so start the journey to becoming great. Allow the transformation process to reshape the school and become more student-centered, teacher-driven, parent-involved, and community-supported.

TRANSFORMATIVE IDEAS FROM THE FIELD

There is a countless number of schools that have either started the transformation process or have completed the transformation process. At the same time, numerous schools have either stopped the transformation process or failed to transform. The difference between the schools that experience success and those that fail to change is often the school's leadership and systems.

Though school transformation should be a team approach, school principals carry a lot of the responsibility to ensure that the transformation is successful. School principals must lead the process from the beginning to end, making sure that the changes that are occurring are targeted, needed, and result in student success. Additionally, school leaders must ensure that stakeholders have opportunities to lead and provide input, which will lead to increased commitment for change success.

School principals must regularly communicate the progress of changes to stakeholders throughout the transformative journey. Communication and transparency are essential to helping the school to overcome challenges, setbacks, and barriers. As information is shared with stakeholders, they become involved in the transformation and begin to embrace the change. Challenges can strengthen the outcomes for the school if embraced.

Challenges often derail the transformative journey; however, visionary school principals use challenges to help develop systems and protocols that can contribute to improving student success and improve the effectiveness of the school's teaching and learning, as well as the school's leadership capacity. If the challenges are viewed as learning opportunities and not barriers, the transformation process will continue and be effective.

PRINCIPAL'S NOTE

*"Transformation is a process, and as life happens
there are tons of ups and downs. It's a journey of
discovery—there are moments on mountaintops and
moments in deep valleys of despair."* —Rick Warren

4 p.m.
September 12
Main Office
Spring Water Elementary School

I closed my door. I was exhausted. I had just completed my first two
weeks as the principal of Spring Water Elementary. My first few weeks
were filled with different meetings with my stakeholder groups. It was
important that I was visible and accessible to them right up front. I did
not want to appear hard to reach or stuck in my office behind closed
doors. The groups I met with were the following:

Parent/Teacher Association
School-site council
English Language Acquisition Committee
Teacher Union Representative
Custodial Staff
Feeder School Administration
Classified Staff

I was conducting these meetings in several ways. Some meetings
were formal with agendas and recorded minutes, while others were
more informal. I met with parents in the parking lot at drop off and pick
up, I chatted with my custodians while helping them clean after lunch,
and talked with teacher aides while they made copies in the office. The
coffee pot was always full and my door was always open to anyone who
wanted to talk.

I also sat down with every teacher individually, giving me the opportunity to get to know them a little better. I also wanted to see if they
would open up to me in the privacy of their classroom with just the two
of us at the table. Some did; others were guarded. I hadn't quite earned
their trust yet. I didn't fault them for their feelings. I knew that building

trust would take time. However, these meetings gave them something that they hadn't had in the past: an outlet.

Experienced principals understand that when you take over a new school, everyone has their own opinion of what is working, what needs to be changed, and who needs to go. I looked back at my notes. Each group took up several pages in my notebook. Main points were starred, highlighted, and circled. I took each main point, idea, reference, and request from each group and wrote them all on my whiteboard. I looked for consistencies, but found more conflicting ideas than agreements.

Even though the school enjoyed high test scores and a strong reputation in the district, it was evident that the organization was at a crossroads. No one particular group was tremendously happy. At the same time, none of them were particularly upset either. There was a feeling of coasting along. For the most part, the seas were calm. The sky was always a shade of bluish grey, never stormy, but never sunny either. There was a general feeling of not wanting to rock the boat to upset any one group.

Leadership is all about taking people on a journey. —Andy Stanley

I looked at my board one more time. I began to look at these diverse points in a different way. They began to look like a road map. This road map needed to be traveled in order to redefine our school's vision. Like any journey, destinations need to be careful planned out, proper supplies need to be packed, and research must be conducted in order to ensure safe travels.

Some of these destinations were very familiar to me. I was already an advocate of utilizing technology to enhance instruction and creating a system of intervention for struggling students. However, some areas were new to me. I had never worked with early literacy before or in an organization with strict disciplinary procedures and rules. Having a strong parent presence on campus was another new venture for me. Over the past two weeks, I had experienced the phenomenon of helicopter parents for the first time.

I wanted to explore each idea, every notion. While I might not agree with each ideal, it was apparent that they were very important to each stakeholder group. I did not want to dismiss or disregard any of their ideas up front. It was important to honor the traditions of the school that had been in place for decades, as several of the teachers had spent their careers at the school and worked with some of the founding teachers.

At the same time, I needed to recognize that there were other teachers who had new ideas that they wanted to try out, but weren't being given the opportunity. In a way, my new school reminded me of the futuristic, yet traditional society of Japan. The country is able to lead the world in forward-thinking ideas and technologies, while not losing its rich cultural heritage. Picture a woman in full kabuki dress and makeup walking down the street in front of massive video arcades and flashing screens.

It was time to go on our journey. Bags were packed with my notes, research, observations, and last but not least, a football helmet. After all, I wanted to be prepared for anything that was tossed my way, both figuratively and literally. Little did I know that I would shortly wear that football helmet at a staff meeting.

TAKEAWAY IDEAS

- School transformation is a journey, not a destination. There will always be room to improve.
- As challenges, setbacks, and obstacles occur, school leaders must help others to remain focused on student success. Student success must always be the primary focus of school transformation.
- The more school leaders, teachers, and staff members embrace change, the more rewarding the transformative journey will be for them professionally. By embracing change, members of the school staff will grow and become better prepared to address the changing needs of students.
- Challenges throughout the transformation process present opportunities for school leaders to develop and acquire new skills that will help move the school forward.
- School leaders must encourage teachers and staff members to take risks to maximize the opportunities to help all students to succeed throughout the transformation process.
- The determination to succeed is critical to the overall effectiveness of the transformative journey.

Chapter Three

Buy-In

Strengthening Opportunities for Success through Engagement

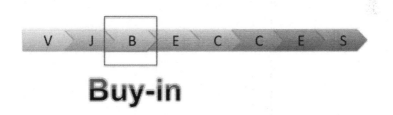

Many school leaders fail to understand the importance of involving stakeholders in developing and carrying out the school's vision. There are schools today where the organizational structure is so rigid that all of the power is centralized to the principal's office. School transformation seeks to empower school leaders to share the decision-making authority with others, which will reduce the complexities that currently face schools. In essence, transformation seeks to "bend" organizational, instructional, cultural, and leadership constructs that prevent a shared leadership approach in schools.

Allowing others to have a voice in the school's vision and journey will lead to buy-in to the school's goals and purpose. When school leaders isolate or silence voices, derailment of the school's transformation is almost certain. As school transformation will lead to major changes in and throughout the school, school leaders must ensure that all voices are heard, valued, and included in the journey.

TRANSFORMATION CORE IDEA

School transformation becomes more meaningful for stakeholders through *buy-in* opportunities. Diverse perspectives strengthen the overall results of the transformation process.

When stakeholders have a voice in their journey, they are more willing to commit to the change process. School transformation will prove to be difficult at times; however, when stakeholders are committed to the change process, difficulties will give way to successes and accomplishments. As more stakeholders become engaged in the transformation process, perspectives and ideas are diversified, which only strengthens and improves the process. To maximize the transformation efforts to change the school's organization and culture, resulting in positive outcomes for students, school leaders will need to establish the expectation that stakeholder buy-in is a critical element throughout the change process.

TRANSFORMATIVE KEY UNDERSTANDINGS

- *Team*—make the transformation process a team effort—stakeholders are more willing to buy-in to the process if others are also engaged.
- *Commitment*—engaging stakeholders in the decision-making process leads to commitment to the overall transformation goals.
- *Importance*—make school transformation important to others by rewriting change in their terms.
- *Beginning*—concentrate on building buy-in before beginning the transformation process.
- *Relationships and Trust*—focus on building relationships with stakeholders that will also lead to mutual trust. Both relationships and trust can help to increase buy-in. Stakeholders are more willing to engage in the transformation process with leaders they have a positive relationship with and also trust.
- *Make teachers and staff members feel important*—instead of leading the change process, empower others to be leaders, which will lead to engagement.

TRANSFORMATIVE ROLES

School Leaders:

- Create opportunities for teachers and staff members to be part of the decision-making process;
- Embrace and celebrate diverse ideas and perspectives;
- Establish the expectation of shared decision-making;
- Be willing to make changes in order to increase stakeholder buy-in and commitment to the transformation process.

Teachers and Staff Members:

- Be willing to offer opinions and ideas to strengthen the transformation process;
- Communicate support for the transformation process through active engagement;
- Seek opportunities to bring perspectives from other stakeholders not at the table;
- Offer ideas that will push the boundaries and comfort zones. Offer constructive criticism of the transformation process in order to strengthen the change within the school for students.
- Be willing to serve as leaders throughout the transformation process and create opportunities where others can be empowered to be leaders.

RESEARCH AND TRANSFORMATION

The first step in school transformation and being a transformative school leader is to recognize the value of stakeholders. School leaders must regularly model for others the importance of taking the time to say thank you, which, as top organizational leaders have found, goes a long way. The opportunity to be school leaders, especially at this point, is a blessing and school leaders must be prepared to embrace the opportunity. Students today need school leaders, teachers, and staff members to recognize their importance in their pursuit to achieve. Furthermore, students need school leaders who are grateful for the opportunity to lead.

Too many school leaders want the title but not the responsibility. Too often, school leaders choose not to lead the charge to create the best school for students. But in today's schools, change is no longer optional; leaders must ignite the call for change to occur now. Throughout the transformation process, it will be important for school leaders to understand how important stakeholder buy-in is to the outcome of school transformation.

According to Farmer, Slater, and Wright (1998), the leader's ability to effectively communicate the organization's vision determines the level of buy-in from staff. Support from staff and stakeholders is essential to effectively changing the organization. School leaders, from time to time, must recognize how much support they have to reach their goal to transform the school. They must recognize that they need others in order to create meaningful change in their school.

School leaders must realize that schools only experience success and transformation because of the support from all stakeholders. Though the school may experience a high level of success, its success is a celebration of stakeholders' support and collaboration. In their research, Parish, Cadwallader, and Busch (2008) found that employer and employee relationships have a positive effect on change processes. Positive relationships lead to greater buy-in among all stakeholders.

Employees (and stakeholders) will embrace change and buy-in to the vision for change if they have a positive relationship with the organizational leader. In other words, school leaders must form relationships with stakeholders in order to create the change needed in schools. A school is only as strong as its community support, and the same can be said about the community. The community will only be as strong as its schools. Two-way support is essential to the school's transformation. No matter the size of the school or the community, support is always the key ingredient to success.

John Maxwell says, "It's better for you to say it than for someone to whisper it," in regards to saying thank you. But giving thanks does not stop with the community, parent/guardians, or the faculty and staff. School leaders must recognize how much they are thankful for students. School leaders, teachers, and staff members rarely understand how critical students are to the success of their transformative journey. At the end of the day, if schools didn't have students, there would be no need for a school. Students should always be the priority of the decision-making in schools.

Evaluate your current school. How often do you stop and tell students "thank you"? For many this will raise the question, why? For others, saying thank you will spark the understanding that we all must be grateful for students for entrusting us with their learning and futures. Too many educators and educational leaders take for granted that students are required to attend school. Schools can no longer afford not to recognize the need to appreciate students. There is an old saying: "The deepest craving of human nature is the need to be appreciated." The same is true throughout the transformation process.

Students in an age of high-stakes testing must be valued for their role in the school. Furthermore, schools must continue to shift from doing things to students and move to doing things with students. Schools must continue to provide students a voice in classrooms, in schools, and in every school district. Student voice is powerful and can be transformative if it is used to create a school that is student-centered.

Students today not only want to have a voice in deciding the direction of their learning, but they expect to have a voice. School leaders must realize that educators today far too often prescribe remedies to student learning before understanding the needs of each student individually. As mentioned earlier, the transformation process focuses on individualizing the learning process and seeking to make sure that each student's needs and goals are addressed.

Schools today must recommit to the idea and principle that students are the reason to look forward to each day. Student success must be the number-one priority for every school, and each school's vision must be aligned to this priority. Public education today is out of time; political and societal forces are demanding results. Though the majority of public schools are doing phenomenal things each day, but there are some public schools that need to change and change quickly. Throughout the transformation process, school leaders must continually reinforce the appreciation for every stakeholder in the school.

The transformation will not be easy and will push some to their limits and well past their zones of comfort, which is all the more reason for school leaders to tell teachers, staff members, and students how they are proud of them and how they appreciate each member of the team. Appreciation results in increased effort, engagement, and empowerment throughout the transformation process. With every obstacle faced, recognize every success, incremental or great. Appreciation and recognition lead to stakeholder buy-in, which leads to transformation.

TRANSFORMATIVE POINTS TO CONSIDER

- Without buy-in, school leaders become ineffective and risk derailing the transformative journey.
- Transformation emphasizes collaboration and shared decision-making, which will help change the school in many ways. The key ingredient to both collaboration and shared decision-making is buy-in, allowing others to be involved in the school process and finding ways to engage others in the transformative process.
- Buy-in helps to transform a school where teachers and school administrators work in isolation, to a school that operates as a team, working toward the same goals and vision.
- Buy-in is more than just asking teachers, staff members, and stakeholders questions, like "Do you support this idea?" Instead, buy-in starts with a shared vision to transform the school and intensely engages everyone in creating a school that students want to attend and others want to be part of.
- Buy-in must also include students—students must be part of the transformative process, as well as, the focus of the transformation process.

PRACTICAL INTRODUCTION

School transformation often fails because school leaders think that they, alone, can transform the school. As we continue to stress, transformation (change) is hard and should not be attempted by the school leader alone. To truly change the school culture and processes, all stakeholders need to be part of the transformation. When we say all, yes we mean students, teachers, staff members, parents/guardians, and members of the community.

It is important for school leaders to work closely with all stakeholders to develop a plan for transformation that is aligned to the school's vision. Involving all stakeholders in the process will result in an effective transformative outcome for students. Buy-in is key to transforming the school from the inside out. Each school can change, but only those schools with a culture of collaboration will succeed.

School transformation is strengthened when stakeholders have buy-in and ownership of the process. School leaders must engage stakeholders in developing a common vision for the school and transformation, as well as developing the change plan. School leaders need stakeholders to take ownership of the transformation process and see change through a positive lens. The more stakeholders own the process, the more they are committed to ensuring success, which results in more positive outcomes for students.

The change process ultimately is about changing the school's operations, vision, culture, structures, processes, and the teaching and learning process. Therefore, stakeholders must have a voice and be committed. To achieve high levels of commitment from stakeholders requires school leaders to create opportunities for stakeholder voices to be heard.

KEY QUESTIONS

The Key Questions are meant to help school leaders begin thinking about the transformation principles in relation to their schools.

- How are stakeholders encouraged to provide a voice in the decision-making process?
- How is collaboration encouraged between school leaders, teachers, and staff members? And with other school stakeholders?
- How often are teachers, staff members, and other stakeholders provided an opportunity to be part of the decision-making process and developing/ evaluating the school's vision and long-term goals?
- Discuss, from your perspective, how allowing stakeholders to weigh in on day-to-day decisions, long-term goals, and the development of the school's vision strengthens your leadership.
- How are students involved in the transformation process?

BUY-IN TRANSFORMED

Buy-in, though often overlooked or undervalued, is a critical component in the transformation process. With the complexities that schools face, along with the challenges of transforming, buy-in will only grow in necessity. The journey to transforming schools can be strengthened when school leaders initiate processes that will encourage engagement of, and buy-in from, stakeholders. Specifically, school leaders must focus on creating opportunities where stakeholders have a voice in the direction of the school.

Also, school leaders must show stakeholders that they value their input and need their buy-in throughout the transformation process. As mentioned in chapter 1, the more stakeholders are involved in creating the school's vision, the more likely they will understand the tenets of the vision and ultimately support the overall goals of the school. The school's vision must drive the school's commitment to garnering support and buy-in from all stakeholders throughout the transformation process.

Strategy: Collaborate

> "Remodeling an organization to capitalize on the advantages of collaboration starts with buy-in from the top."
>
> —SayQuotable

Many of the organizations we view as great, effective, and profitable have similar characteristics. We all know the common characteristics that we often associate with "effective" organizations; they have the best leaders, top talent, and a culture of innovation. In fact, all of the organizations that we think of as effective obviously have effective leaders, committed employees, and a culture of success and innovation. But they also have something that schools can learn from: a culture of collaboration. High-performing organizations, like high-performing schools, have a culture of collaboration and view silos as the enemy of being great.

Establishing a culture of collaboration is an essential component that will lead to stakeholder engagement and buy-in. Throughout the transformation process that occurs in schools, collaboration usually is synonymous with stakeholder buy-in. Schools, like other organizations, need commitment and buy-in from stakeholders. Buy-in leads to commitment to the school's vision and plan for transformation. Additionally, buy-in helps to encourage collaboration between stakeholders. As the school continues the transformation journey, collaboration will be a critical change component.

Collaboration helps to create a culture in schools that encourages innovation, risk-taking, and that is focused on student success. We find that schools that have a strong, positive, and collaborative culture have higher levels of student success. High student achievement is not surprising as all stakeholders are rowing in the same direction; that is, by working together they can help all students experience success. A culture of collaboration is essential to the school transforming and becoming student-centered.

Specifically, collaboration leads to new ways in teaching and learning, innovation in the classroom and throughout the school, and risk-taking. Schools must begin to take strategic and calculated risks to move student achievement. Complacency is a brutal enemy to success and is often "stealth like," working behind the scenes in organizations and schools. By embracing innovation and collaboration, schools keep moving, challenging the status quo, and preventing attitudes of complacency from forming.

Collaboration helps school administrators, teachers, and staff members to be comfortable taking risks, as they realize that supports are there to assist them as they step out of their comfort zones and possibly stumble. Just like in Fortune 500 companies, which succeed through innovation and risk-taking, schools need networks of supports that first begin with colleagues in their buildings.

Schools must also have school leaders who value teachers and staff members who are willing to push the limits, who embrace the diverse perspectives in and throughout the decision-making process, as well as value risk-taking as a means to move the needle for student success. Many schools fail to continue to move forward as a result of complacency. Just as schools experience success, they experience failure as a result of not realizing the negative results of standing still.

School leaders must encourage teachers and staff members to collaborate. By creating a culture of collaboration, student success will only continue to increase, which is the ultimate goal of our work as educators. Furthermore, by encouraging collaboration in our schools, school leaders limit the possibilities of remaining still or moving backward in their pursuit to transform and become more student-centered.

According to Peter M. Senge, a senior lecturer at the Massachusetts Institute of Technology's School of Management, "Collaboration is vital to sustain what we call profound or really deep change, because without it, organizations are just overwhelmed by the forces of the status quo." Senge provides a clear understanding of why collaboration is critical in all schools. As student success increases, as a result of the transformation process, the status quo will only lead to the same result and actually begin to move student achievement backward.

Furthermore, Senge encourages educators to continue to look for ways to energize the learning process and seek innovative strategies to improve instructional strategies. By committing to transform the school, school leaders, teachers, and staff members opt to push the limits. School transformation encourages collaboration and removes the fear of failure. In highly collaborative, high-performing schools, failures are viewed as opportunities to grow, not setbacks.

Change is hard, but, when embraced, will lead to great things for students. Innovative collaboration encourages school leaders, teachers, and staff members to look outside of the normal classroom walls to find new opportunities to improve the teaching and learning process. Each day, collaboration is a focus of school leaders as they seek to transform the school by removing silos that impede student achievement and creating a collaborative school culture.

Strategy: Establish Professional Learning Communities (PLCs)

"If you want to go fast, go alone. If you want to go far, go together."

—African Proverb

Great organizations succeed as a result of establishing a culture of collaboration. School leaders, teachers, and staff members must work together to move the school forward. Furthermore, school leaders must emphasize the need to encourage buy-in of stakeholders through collaborative leadership structures and processes that encourage shared decision-making. When school leaders model the expectation that all voices are critical in the transformation process and actively seek and value buy-in from all stakeholders, then a culture of collaboration develops.

School transformation is not about how fast you arrive at your goals, but instead, about creating systems and structures that will lead to increases in student success for the long-term. Furthermore, throughout the transformation process there will be a emphasis on creating a culture that is based on collaboration to increase student success. Student success must always be the primary and guiding purpose in all school decisions and functions.

The journey to transforming the way the school does business will be intense, full of barriers, but also rewarding in the end for the school and for students. Schools that have successfully transformed have seen increases in student success and improvements in morale, community support, and culture optimization. As schools decide to go through the change process, student success through emphasizing buy-in and collaboration of stakeholders will only grow in need.

Helping all students to succeed must be shared, collectively. Collaboration and stakeholder buy-in must be emphasized from the beginning. Schools that go through the transformation process must move away from working and teaching in silos and move toward a culture where collaborative teaching is the standard. Furthermore, learning must become more personalized and collaborative.

The culture of a high-performing and transformed school is characterized by a shared focus and collaboration, which is achieved by emphasizing buy-in from all stakeholders. These characteristics must also be present in all class-rooms. Just as the school and school-wide culture must reflect collaboration and buy-in, so must each classroom also exhibit these same characteristics.

All classrooms must have a laser focus on ensuring all students experience success (a shared focus). If teachers and staff members work to encourage student buy-in in classrooms, then the sky is truly the only limit to student success. School leaders model the expectation that buy-in is important and valued in school, along with collaboration. This focus and emphasis on buy-in must go all the way down to the classroom, where teachers and staff create opportunities for students to buy-in to the transformation process.

School leaders, teachers, and staff members must be planning together, observing each other, identifying areas for improvement as a team, and using professional learning communities to move the school to the next level. Additionally, there must be an emphasis on including students in the decision-making process. Though student voice is rarely emphasized, student buy-in and shared leadership among students and teachers are hallmarks of transformed schools.

School leaders, teachers, and staff members in transformed schools real-ize how important buy-in and collaboration are in pushing the limits. As a team, school leaders, teachers, and staff members must look for and create opportunities to collaborate and structures that encourage diverse perspec-tives throughout the decision-making process. Collaboration is the essence of buy-in.

The school's success, by opting to transform, will be determined by its ability to move individual students to a higher level. But to be clear, don't think the work ever becomes easier. The transformation process from the be-ginning and end will be difficult, challenging but also rewarding. The trans-formation process encourages schools to develop and utilize professional learning communities effectively.

Often school leaders, teachers, and staff members indicate that they "do" PLCs. But their responses indicate otherwise. In our opinion and experience, professional learning communities are more about the school's culture than a system. When schools have a culture of collaboration, professional learning communities are the product or the result. School leaders, teachers, and staff members come to expect collaboration and buy-in.

High-performing schools have professional learning communities that are engrained in the school's culture and systems; they are where school leaders, teachers, and staff members collaborate openly, daily, and strategically to move student success. Often, school leaders, teachers, and staff members talk about systems of collaboration without ever mentioning the purpose: student success. Professional learning communities are mentioned in the buy-in section to emphasize, yet again, how collaboration and buy-in are so closely connected.

When a school has a positive culture of collaboration, this is a good indication that stakeholders are committed to the school's vision and journey. There is an unspoken expectation throughout the transformation process that buy-in is essential to truly changing the school. Structural change, where the school's DNA is changed for the better, will not occur without the buy-in from all stakeholder groups.

Transformation is no simple process and due to the increasing complexities that face schools, buy-in and professional learning communities must be a part of the school's strategy and also the fabric of the change process. To help students reach higher levels of success, professional learning communities are growing in necessity. School leaders, teachers, and staff members must freely and regularly collaborate together to find new ways to help engage students in the learning process, which will lead to even higher levels of success for students.

Teachers and staff members must be encouraged to collaborate even more, team-teach, plan together, team-tutor before or after school, and so much more. It is important that stakeholders, through professional learning communities, work together to move the student success needle. Furthermore, to radically change the structures within school to have all arrows pointing to student success as the focal point, school-wide collaboration is a necessity.

Together, as a team, student achievement can increase, if school leaders, teachers, and staff members collectively push the boundaries and challenge the status quo. If educators keep doing the same thing and getting the same result, then they will never reach their goals, nor will students reach the levels of success that are attainable. High-performing schools are the model for pushing the boundaries and embracing the differentiation of strategies in order to meet the needs of their students.

School leaders, teachers, and staff members in high-performing and transformed schools are not afraid to scrap old plans and develop new ones if it will lead to growth in student success. Collaboratively, through the school's culture of professional learning, they work together, seeking buy-in from all stakeholders, to identify trends in data that will result in better strategies that will help students (data-driven shared decision-making).

School leaders must understand how complex the teaching and learning process is today, and how complex transforming a school is. They must utilize professional learning communities to lead improvements throughout the school. Collaboration is a strategy that is powerful and transcending. When school leaders communicate the expectation of collaboration, it transcends ideologies and becomes the norm throughout the school.

Professional learning communities provide a great arena to have open, transparent, and crucial conversations about the transformation process, empowerment, student success, and so many other things. But even more than conversations, professional learning communities actually provide an arena to perform the actual work necessary to transform the school. School leaders must communicate the expectation that professional learning communities are free zones open for discussion, diverse viewpoints, decisions, and respect.

Professional collaboration and stakeholder buy-in are essential to creating a professional learning community. Professional learning communities foster a culture of individual and team continuous growth as educators and administrators. Schools must continue to focus on team power throughout the transformation process. School transformation will not occur if it is done by one individual or a group of individuals; it must be a team approach.

Joel Osteen, a best-selling author and minister, says, "By ourselves we're strong, but together, we're unstoppable." The transformation process is important and will consume a lot of resources and time in schools. School leaders must unite teachers and staff, along with other stakeholders, working together in order to have a positive outcome. The days of operating behind closed doors or in silos are obsolete.

Teams must embrace challenges together and help one another to overcome obstacles, barriers, and setbacks. Educators must not be afraid to identify improvement priorities and next steps; all great organizations have room to grow. Again, all school leaders must create opportunities where all stakeholders can collaborate freely and strategize to find ways to improve student success. Remember what President Lyndon Johnson once said, "There are no problems we cannot solve together, and very few that we can solve by ourselves."

Strategy: Practice Affirmation

> "It's the small little things that make all the difference not just receiving or noticing them but giving them."
>
> —Affirmed Life

School transformation is hard and will take its toll on everyone involved. As schools begin to push the boundaries, school leaders must realize the importance of affirming the work of teachers and staff members in the school. Affirmation, the recognition of good work by stakeholders, leads to their buy-in of the school's vision, goals, and journey. Often, school leaders become so busy with day-to-day operations and leading that they forget to affirm teachers' and staff members' quality of work.

An effective strategy to show affirmation of work is by giving teachers and staff members the autonomy to make school-wide decisions. School leaders must show that they value the work and decisions of teachers and staff members throughout the transformative process. Teachers must work diligently to help other teachers and staff members push the boundaries and also be change agents in the school. Furthermore, they must create processes that will encourage buy-in from all stakeholders. This starts by publicly recognizing the work of teachers and staff members and their dedication to student success. Affirming the work of others throughout the transformative process leads to buy-in of others and commitment to the goal: student success.

TRANSFORMATIVE IDEAS FROM THE FIELD

The number of effective school leaders continues to decrease with each passing academic year. There are many reasons why school leaders continue to struggle with leading in today's schools, but one in particular is buy-in. As school leaders, we continue to make the cardinal mistake of not providing opportunities for others to lend a voice in the school's direction. We, school leaders, are too quick to make decisions without involving others in developing a plan.

As a result, schools often find themselves going through cycles of defeat, which leads to low morale among school stakeholders, teacher and staff turnover, and ultimately the school leader(s) throwing in the towel or being removed. Fortunately, there is hope for school leaders who want to truly transform the school. We find in high-performing organizations a key ingredient that can be transferred to schools: buy-in. Buy-in is free and it carries a lot of rewards for the school and the school leader. Transformative school leaders practice regularly seeking input from others and encouraging others to provide feedback.

In fact, garnering buy-in from stakeholders is not something that they do; it is actually programmed into their leadership style and part of their visionary DNA. Those school leaders in turn help to instill collaboration into the fabric of the school culture, which requires buy-in and engagement of stakeholders throughout the school. This is when change truly takes place in school; when everyone feels like they are critical (buy-in) to the vision, the journey, and the school transformation.

PRINCIPAL'S NOTES

"Deep and sustainable change . . . requires changes in behavior among those who do not welcome the change." —Douglas Reeves

11:45 a.m.
October
Staff Lunch Room
Spring Water Elementary School

I had learned from my various conversations that change was desired by many stakeholders. There was, however, a small, but strong contingency of teachers who wanted to keep the school rooted in history, traditions, and structure. It would be with this group of teachers that I would have to do the most work. I learned early on in my career that you can't convince a group of teachers to change by talking to them.

They have seen every educational initiative under the sun come and go, along with the school leaders who tried to implement them. I needed these teachers at my table. They needed to see that I was on their side, not against them. It was important to acknowledge that we both wanted the same thing: to provide the best educational opportunity for our students as possible. By letting them know that we were all on the same side, I was able to put to bed the notion that I didn't respect their hard work over the past several decades.

I spent a good chuck of my day observing their instruction and interactions with students. I often went to them for advice and guidance that required the knowledge of a teacher who had been around the block a few times. I learned a lot during these observations. History is important. To know where you are going, you must know where you have been. Some of these teachers had spent the bulk of their career at the school. Principals need to honor that commitment, work, and dedication. I also learned that they were excellent teachers, truly accomplished in their craft.

Therefore, I asked several of them to be a part of my leadership team.

First, they were shocked.

Then, they were delighted.

Teachers who wanted change were surprised as well, although confused that I would jeopardize our chances of moving forward as a school with bringing these other teachers onboard the leadership team. I understood their fear. However, I needed to have both sides come together so that we could solidify our new vision, moving the school in a new direction while maintaining traditions and history.

Our first few leadership meetings were tense. I could sense that these two sides did not see eye-to-eye on many issues. In order to keep our train heading in the right direction, I ensured that our vision statement was a part of each and every conversation. Then things got better. The team acted more clinically and less critically. Compromises were made and different viewpoints were taken into consideration. We used more inclusive words such as "we" and "ours," rather than "I" and "me."

As the group gelled, it was time to bring our new initiatives and ideas to the rest of the staff. I knew that if I alone carried this message that it would be looked upon as my idea and my idea alone. The message would be better received coming from the staff's colleagues. We chose a staff meeting to present these new initiatives with the caveat that they were all works in progress and nothing would be finished without full consensus from the staff.

This notion was met with surprise and optimism as they were used to just being told what to do in the past. I presented the big picture ideas and limitations, but left the details and the demonstrations to teachers on the leadership team. I carefully recorded feedback from teachers to ensure that they knew that their viewpoints were being heard. I again heard the shift in language from "I" and "me" to "we" and "ours." The staff felt that they had fully participated in the discussion and had their viewpoints integrated into the new ideas and initiatives.

In the past, the staff had felt that school-wide decisions were solely in the hands of the leadership. These decisions were always made behind closed doors and were told to the staff after final decisions were made.

Now, they felt empowered.

TAKEAWAY IDEAS

- Create opportunities where stakeholders have a voice in the transformation process.
- Define transformation in terms that all stakeholders can understand and relate to.
- Make buy-in a critical component in the school's success. Constantly reinforce the importance of buy-in throughout the decision-making process.
- Buy-in will help to create a culture of collaboration in school.

Chapter Four

Empowerment

Increasing Social Capital through Collaboration

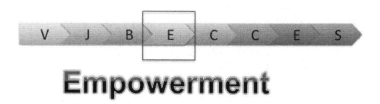

Empowerment

Jim Goodnight, the founder and CEO of SAS, understands that employees and customers are essential to the overall success and health of the organization. Goodnight has taken SAS from a small data and technology company in North Carolina, to a global leader in data analytics. Empowering others to be leaders throughout the organization has been key to his company's success. As school leaders, we can learn a valuable lesson from Goodnight's approach to leadership: empowerment sends a clear signal that all stakeholders play a critical role in the overall success of the school. In other words stakeholder empowerment is vision critical.

As schools begin the transformation process, stakeholders must be empowered to be leaders, change agents, and risk takers in the school. Empowerment, when mentioned in education, usually means empowering others to be leaders; empowerment is so much more than just leadership. Throughout this chapter, we focus our attention on empowering others to be leaders, but we want to emphasize that empowerment is much more than shared decision-making and collaborative leadership structures.

Goodnight's leadership style guides our thinking that empowerment in schools is about empowering stakeholders to aspire to be leaders for students, taking risks, thinking outside the box, and doing whatever it takes to move student success to the next level. School leaders must empower others to push the limits within schools and be change agents committed to transforming the school to become a student-centered learning organization.

TRANSFORMATIVE IDEA

School transformation is strengthened by the empowerment of stakeholders throughout the process. Empowerment of stakeholders helps to improve the effectiveness of the school's leadership, instructional effectiveness, and outcomes for students.

Empowerment of others to be leaders always strengthens the organization and the journey. The purpose of school transformation is to improve student success. Improvements in student success and preparedness for the next level are accomplished by creating collaborative leadership structures, where stakeholders are empowered to be part of the decision-making process. As teachers and staff members are empowered to be leaders, they in turn empower students to be leaders of their own learning. The possibilities for student outcomes and positive changes in the school's organization are only increased by empowering stakeholders to be leaders in schools.

TRANSFORMATIVE KEY UNDERSTANDINGS

- *School-wide*—empowerment must be present in all school processes, not just throughout the transformation process.
- *Culture*—Empowerment of stakeholders to be leaders and change agents must be part of the school's culture (DNA).
- *Authentic leadership*—school transformation requires stakeholders to have authentic leadership opportunities where teachers and staff members can be innovative, take risks, and actively be engaged in the decision-making process.
- *Structural*—the transformation process requires that traditional leadership structures give way to collaborative leadership structures, which are characterized by collaboration and teamwork.
- *Students*—Throughout the transformation process, students become empowered to be leaders of their own learning and provide a voice in the school's direction and decision-making process. The goal is actively engaging students in a teaching and learning process that is relevant, rigorous, and student-centered.

- *Continuous Pursuit*—as the school transforms processes and empowers stakeholders to be actively engaged in the school transformation, there will need to be a focus on continuous empowerment. That is, seeking new opportunities to sustain empowerment and be strategic about how stakeholders are empowered. As schools change, so does empowerment.

TRANSFORMATIVE ROLES

School Leaders:

- Recognize how empowerment of others throughout the transformation process strengthens the overall school leadership and results in positives for student success;
- Create opportunities where teachers, staff members, and other stakeholders can be change leaders;
- Establish the expectation and need for empowerment of students in the transformation process;
- Develop structures that encourage collaborative, decision-making processes throughout the transformation process.

Teachers and Staff Members:

- Advocate for opportunities to be change leaders throughout the transformation process;
- Create opportunities for students to be "leaders of their own learning";
- Embrace all opportunities to be leaders in the change process;
- Seek opportunities to grow leadership skills that are aligned to the vision and goals of the transformation process.

RESEARCH AND TRANSFORMATION

Empowerment should not be underestimated. As stakeholders are empowered to be leaders in an organization and part of the decision-making process, their commitment to the organization's goals is strengthened. Empowerment leads to engagement, which leads to increased performance on many different levels. Coquyt and Creasman (2017) emphasize that collaborative leadership, empowerment of teachers to be leaders in school, is not only needed in today's schools, but essential to addressing the many complexities found in schools.

As current and former school leaders, we have seen the performance increase first-hand in schools that have an active, positive, and empowering culture. According to GanijiNia, Gilaninia, Sharami, and PoorAli (2013), employee empowerment is one of the most effective ways to increase performance. As schools engage in transformation, school leaders will need to empower others to be part of the decision-making process, which will strengthen the overall outcomes of the change process. As the transformation occurs in the school, the complexities will only continue to grow.

Nixon (1994) states it best when he says that organizations are regularly facing uncertainties. These uncertainties are only compounded as change begins. To overcome these unknowns, Nixon (1994) argues that organizations must seek to empower stakeholders instead of controlling them. Schools can no longer operate under rigid organizational structures that limit stakeholder leadership roles and chances to lend a voice to the school's long-term decisions. There is a growing and intense need for school leaders to find ways to engage others in leading the school, especially throughout the transformation process.

Employee empowerment is well researched (Yukl and Becker, 2012). Based on the research that shows positive trends when employees are empowered, school leaders should be comfortable in empowering stakeholders, including students. Student leadership opportunities throughout the transformation process are plentiful. The students must only be given the opportunities to embrace the chance to lead. There should be no question about how student voice is a positive addition to the change process. School leaders must quickly address questions about why student voice is needed in the transformation process.

School leaders must consistently and regularly communicate the need to empower students throughout the transformation process. School leaders must remind all stakeholders that transformation is in fact about creating a school that is more student-centered and empowering for students. Though empowerment has many positive advantages, one distinct advantage is that it strengthens the overall school leadership. According to Freire and Fernandes (2015), stakeholders who are empowered trust their school leaders more and support their vision for the school. As school leaders empower others, they, in turn, strengthen their ability to make and lead the change needed to create a student-centered school.

Empowerment, particularly throughout the change process, may seem threatening to many school leaders, including teachers, staff members, and students. Though change does push many out of their comfort zones, empowerment must be embraced as a strategic tool to create the foundation for long-term, sustainable change. As a school leader, you must not fear that empowerment challenges your authority, but instead, should embrace empowerment as a tool to strengthen the school's ability to become student-focused.

TRANSFORMATIVE POINTS TO CONSIDER

- School administrators are too quick to overlook how empowerment can propel a school from the bottom to the top. Empowerment is the secret ingredient to transforming a school culture, which then transforms the school from the inside.
- Think about how school principals want to be empowered to make district-level decisions. The same feeling is shared by teachers, staff, and students. They too want to be empowered to be leaders in school, just like school principals want to be empowered to be leaders in the district.
- No matter what anyone says, school principals do not have unlimited resources of energy. The job is becoming increasingly overwhelming. To keep the ship (the school) moving in the right direction, it is in our best interest and the interest of students to empower others to be navigators on this incredible journey called school.
- Empowerment is discussed in terms of something new, but in fact, educators have been talking about empowerment for decades; yet, school administrators continue to struggle with sharing leadership with others. Why is that? The reason is many school leaders fail to see the benefits empowerment has on student achievement and, more importantly, their tenure as school principals.

PRACTICAL INTRODUCTION

The school transformation process is the perfect time to empower others to be leaders in the school. As mentioned earlier, the school transformation process requires a high level of stakeholder buy-in (or engagement) so that the school leader does not shoulder the entire responsibility for success. Additionally, empowerment, the ability of others to be leaders in school, leads to a higher level of engagement and buy-in of stakeholders in the school. Likewise, empowerment leads to more ownership of the school's decisions and vision. School leaders build support for their leadership and vision as they empower others.

Empowerment of others is key to creating a sustainable transformation process. Empowering others along the transformation journey strengthens the process. No matter the organization or change plan, stakeholders want to be able to lead, have a voice in the decision-making process, and, more importantly, have the opportunity to serve others. Isolation or self-serving decisions have no place throughout the transformation process.

By school leaders empowering stakeholders and giving them the opportunity to lead, they create a culture that prevents isolation, by establishing an expectation of transparent decision-making, student-centered decisions, and collaborative leadership. School leaders must do more than just pay lip service to empowerment. They must not only communicate an expectation that all stakeholders are empowered to be leaders in the school, but also model the empowerment of others. Genuine empowerment expands the school's leadership capacity to bring about the needed change for students.

In addition, genuine empowerment trickles down to the student level. Often forgotten throughout the empowerment process, students need to have a voice in the direction of the school—since they must be the primary focus of all schools. Known by many as the only time the trickle-down theory actually works, when teachers are empowered, they in turn, empower students to be leaders of their own learning. School transformation cannot occur in schools that limit leadership roles to a select few. School transformation needs a bench full of leaders who are ready to step up to the plate and become change agents.

KEY QUESTIONS

The Key Questions are meant to help school leaders begin thinking about the transformation principles in relation to their schools.

- What is the current situation in school? How are stakeholders empowered to be leaders, change agents, or risk-takers in school?
- How are stakeholders empowered to be student-centered?
- How does empowerment align with the school's vision? Vision for transformation? How does empowerment help to transform the school?
- What supports are in place that will help to create a culture of empowerment?
- How does empowerment help to strengthen the school's leadership capacity?
- How does empowerment align to the school's strategic plan?
- What are the empowerment components in the school?

EMPOWERMENT TRANSFORMED

Strategy: Make Sure to Recognize Stakeholders, as They Are Taking Risks and Pushing the Limits

"Leaders should influence others in such a way that it builds people up, encourages and educates them so they can duplicate attitude in others."

—Bob Goshen

As school leaders look to encourage others to become leaders throughout the teaching and learning process, stakeholders will need to be praised and recognized as they assume leadership roles. Identifying and supporting stakeholders as they lead projects, facilitate professional learning communities, and become leaders in other capacities, will help them develop the confidence to lead going forward. Furthermore, recognizing stakeholders for their leadership also sends the message that their leadership is in alignment with the overall goals and vision for the school and transformation.

Strategy: Create Opportunities Where Stakeholders Are Empowered to Be Leaders

"If your actions create a legacy that inspires others to dream more, learn more, do more and become more, then, you are an excellent leader."

—Dolly Parton

The best way for stakeholders to be become leaders is through experience. For the leadership bench to grow, school leaders must be open to creating opportunities for others to develop and acquire the skills necessary to be effective leaders. Creating opportunities for others to be leaders in school sends the message that the school leadership is focused on empowerment, collaboration, and shared decision-making. Additionally, empowering others to lead also sends a message that school leadership is transparent and open to the exchange of information with others.

Strategy: Develop a Transformative Mindset

"The task of a leader is the leader is to get his people from where they are to where they have not been."

—Henry Kissinger

School leaders must work to develop the transformation mindset in others. The goal is to help others to aspire to be leaders who focus on the positives, potential, and the possibilities within the school. Long-term change needs a strong bench of leaders who are willing to step up to the plate and lead the change even during difficult or uncertain times. We are often asked what the characteristics of a transformational leader are. Below we provide the features of a transformational leader, which also form the basis for a transformational mindset. A transformational leader is:

- Inspirational: A transformational leader inspires others to improve continually, to seek higher levels of performance as a means to improve student success.

- Strategic: A transformational leader makes strategic decisions based on what is in the best interest of students and the organizational performance. They are calculating and help keep the school focused on the overall school strategy: the bigger picture.
- Change-oriented: A transformational leader embraces change and views change as an opportunity to strengthen their leadership and the overall organization.
- Collaborative: A transformational leader seeks and creates opportunities to involve others in the decision-making process through collaborative leadership structures. They view collaboration as an opportunity to engage and empower others to be leaders. Additionally, they utilize collaboration as a means to encourage and engage diverse perspectives in leading the school.
- Visionary: A transformational leader is always thinking about the future. They encourage others to be creative and innovative as a means to create the type of school for students that they all dream of.
- Risk tolerant: A transformational leader takes strategic risks and encourages others to take risks as a means to push the limits of their abilities and the school's abilities.
- Adaptable: A transformational leader adapts to the needs of the students, stakeholders, and school.

Strategy: Freely Share Information and Intelligence

"The most important role of a leader is to set a clear direction, be transparent about how to get there and to stay the course."

—Irene Rosenfeld-Mondelez

School leaders, in order to be transformative, must also be transparent with information and intelligence. Restricting the sharing of information and intelligence only restricts the empowerment of others in the school. Without information, stakeholders would try to become leaders with one hand tied behind their back. School leaders must model transparency, especially in the age of increased accountability at the local, state, and federal levels. Freely sharing information encourages others to be engaged in the transformative process and more willing to go the extra mile throughout the journey.

Strategy: Be a Lifelong Lead Learner

"The key to success is dedication to life-long learning."

—Stephen Covey

There is nothing more empowering than seeing a school leader who is always engaged in professional growth. In high-performing schools, school leaders are involved in professional growth opportunities with aspiring leaders. Transformative school leaders who commit to creating a culture of empowerment also create a culture of continuous improvement, which includes ongoing professional learning for teachers and staff.

There is a key difference, as educators have learned, between professional learning and professional development. Professional learning is typically ongoing, whereas professional development is a single event. School leaders, teachers, and administrators are encouraged to engage in ongoing professional learning as a means to strengthen the school's culture and student outcomes.

School leaders must help others to remain engaged in lifelong learning. As schools continue to increase in complexity, school leaders, teachers, and staff members will need to have a variety of skills, strategies, and tools to meet the changing needs of students. Furthermore, continuous learning also sparks interest in others to become leaders as they acquire the necessary knowledge and skills, and develop an interest in leading.

Education often leads to leadership; that is, continuous learning also helps to ignite leadership interests in others that can aid in the transformation of the school. Lifelong learning demonstrated by school leaders sends the message to teachers, staff members, and other stakeholders that the school is a center of learning, not only for students, but also for the greater school community.

Strategy: Develop an Empowering Blueprint

> "Leadership is about setting a direction. It's about creating a vision, empowering and inspiring people to want to achieve the vision, and enabling them to do so with energy and speed through an effective strategy. In its most basic sense, leadership is about mobilizing a group of people to jump into a better future."
>
> —John P. Kotter

Before school leaders can begin empowering others to be leaders, they must first have a strategy. Empowering stakeholders to be leaders in the school must be aligned to the overall goals of the school, as well as the vision for the school and overall transformation process. The alignment of empowering stakeholders to be leaders and the overall school strategy must be tight, as misalignment can derail the growth process, as well as the transformation process.

Though all great journeys begin by taking the first step, they also start with a good map. Transformation is no different and school leaders would be wise to have a well-developed plan prior to beginning the process. If school leaders fail to identify the vision for transformation, along with a strategy to reach this vision, the results will not be as rewarding. In fact, the results will not be positive for student achievement or the school's overall effectiveness.

Strategy and vision are rarely mentioned in connection with creating a culture of empowerment in schools. But in fact, strategy and vision are critical to the advancement of others to become leaders. School leaders, working closely with others, must develop a school vision, a clear direction that requires a high level of stakeholder empowerment. The complexities that schools face are too much for leadership to be isolated to one individual or the principal's office.

Transformation requires an approach that empowers teachers and staff members to be leaders and change agents in the school. Just as the transformation process must have a blueprint (strategy), so does the empowerment of others to be leaders. Gain an understanding of why empowerment is vision critical to the transformation process. School leaders must first embrace the idea and concept of empowerment before beginning the school's transformation journey.

TRANSFORMATIVE IDEAS FROM THE FIELD

To many school leaders, empowering others to be leaders is a daunting task. As pressures increase for schools to perform, school leaders face an unbelievable level of accountability. Many states still have accountability models that hold school leaders accountable for student performance. In fact, many accountability models, as research shows, work against empowering others to be leaders in the school.

As pressures to perform increase, it will be impossible for school leaders to try to transform schools alone. No matter what accountability model is used, school leaders will need to empower others to be leaders if schools are to be turned into organizations that result in all students succeeding. Empowerment can be transformative in any school and the results are amazing for student achievement.

School leaders must work through existing barriers that prevent empowerment of teachers and staff members to become leaders in the school. The organizational structures typically work against creating a culture of empowerment in schools. Collaboratively, school leaders, teachers, and staff members must identify ways to remove structures that prevent empowerment and collaboration.

Ultimately the goal is to create an empowering school culture that is characterized by a high level of teamwork, moving student success to higher levels and the formation of collaborative leadership structures that aid in the development of empowered stakeholders to be leaders. Effective school leaders realize that they cannot lead alone; in fact, they refuse to have narrowed organizational structures that prevent empowerment and collaboration.

As such, effective school leaders work closely with teachers, staff members, and other stakeholders to transform the school, beginning with an inspiring vision for change. By creating a vision for change, school leaders can embed the need for stakeholder empowerment and the insistence of collaboration and shared-decision making. Empowerment can happen if given the opportunity.

PRINCIPAL'S NOTE

"Empowerment isn't a buzzword among leadership gurus. It's a proven technique where leaders give their teams the appropriate training, tools, resources, and guidance to succeed." —John Rampton

3:30 p.m.
November 17
Computer Lab
Spring Water Elementary School

We had crafted our vision, been on a journey of discovery, and had successfully gotten the staff as a whole to buy-in to new initiatives. Now began the hard part. Theoretical ideas are one thing. Tangible uses of that theoretical knowledge are another. Our ideas for change were rich, complex, and multifaceted. They involved technology, student data, and informed instructional practices. There were a lot of different moving parts that required teachers to have a significant level of training, mastery, and autonomy in order to be successful.

Designing a comprehensive training and support system was going to be essential in order for us to be successful. I didn't mind holding hands in the beginning, but I knew that teachers would have to be able to navigate new systems on their own in order to feel comfortable moving forward. There is nothing worse than hearing, "See . . . I told you this wouldn't work."

I had teachers on all different stages of the learning continuum. Some staff members were completely new to looking at data; others had been doing it for years. Some were comfortable with using our online data information system to navigate through different assessments and scores, while others shuddered at the thought of logging on to a new program.

I knew I had to craft a comprehensive, differentiated, and engaging training model. The first thing I did was to have teachers rate themselves on how comfortable they were with the new tool, and the technology involved with using it. I had several staff members e-mail me telling me how happy they were that we would be splitting up the staff in this way.

My more advanced teachers were concerned that they would have to go through the basics with teachers who struggled with technology. My struggling teachers were worried that they would have to keep up with the more advanced teachers. I ended up with three distinct groups: novice, middle of the road, and advanced. While I was comfortable leading any or all of the groups, I chose to utilize my teacher leaders, as I have found that it makes the training more inclusive and collegial.

The teachers in each group felt comfortable with their colleagues leading the group.

I had also learned from speaking with my staff that they were concerned about receiving ongoing support, not just a one-time training. Therefore, I created a system where teachers could receive training until they felt comfortable with the new tool or if new questions came up.

The teacher leaders served as on-campus experts who were available on a daily basis. After the initial training session, I "graduated" the advanced group and moved up the middle of the road teachers to advanced. My novice group became my middle of the road group. We cycled through until the vast majority of teachers completed the advanced training.

Teachers who still needed more support were given one-on-one training. By using this process, teachers not only felt comfortable in using the new tool to benefit teaching and learning, but felt that they had accomplished something as well. This feeling of accomplishment was magnified in the original novice group ten times over. That feeling of empowerment was something that they hadn't felt in a long time. There was now electricity in the air. Teachers at other schools were wondering if we had put something in the water. The word was out about our school. Change was in the air.

TAKEAWAY IDEAS

- Empowerment begins with an inspiring vision for change that is aligned with the overall school goals.
- Collaboration encourages the empowerment of others to be leaders in the school.
- School leaders must create opportunities that will allow others to be leaders in the school.
- Engagement of others in the decision-making process leads to their empowerment.
- Empowerment requires a commitment to continuous learning to remain valid.
- Empowerment of others to be leaders must be a goal of the transformation process.

Chapter Five

Change

Creating a School Students Need and Want

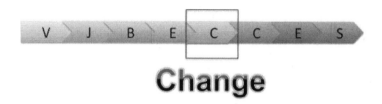

Transformation, at the end of the day, is about changing the school. School transformation is focused on changing the teaching and learning process, leadership structures, strategic focus, or all three and so much more. Several school leaders begin the transformation process as a means to change the school's culture; that is, changing the DNA of the school and the inner workings of the school.

Often, the problems that are found in the school have a lot to do with the culture. Is the school's culture characterized as adult-centered or student-centered, is the school strategic or sporadic, and is the school collaborative or isolated. There are many more characteristics of schools that may need to change, but ultimately what we listed are the primary culture components that are often transformed.

School leaders must work to ensure that the school's culture is a focus throughout the transformation process. We believe that both culture and organizational (school) transformation are interconnected and will occur if done correctly. Often, the organization is what impedes the culture from changing. The school's structures, policies, and protocols play an important role in the school's culture. When teachers or staff members indicate that they struggle to find time to collaborate, to work together, this is a structure issue that must be transformed.

The school's culture can be changed if school leaders, teachers, and staff members work together to identify those things that work against or impede change from occurring. Transforming the way things are done on a daily basis can and will have a positive impact on the school's culture. Remember, culture trumps strategy every time, so it is important for the culture of the school to be considered when blueprinting the school's transformative journey. Change is needed and can happen, if change is understood by all stakeholders.

TRANSFORMATION CORE IDEA

School transformation is about helping the school, leaders, teachers, staff members, and other stakeholders embrace change. Openness and embrace of change are essential to creating the best learning environment and program for students.

> To meet the diverse needs of today's students, schools must radically change the teaching and learning process, as well as the school's organization. Throughout the transformation process, change occurs based on the needs of students and improvements needed in the school to meet the changing dynamics of a twenty-first-century institution of learning. Furthermore, change is needed in order to make learning more personalized and organizational leadership become more flexible and less rigid.

TRANSFORMATIVE KEY UNDERSTANDINGS

- *True Focus*—The school's culture through transformation becomes focused on students, doing whatever it takes to help students succeed.
- *Intensity Level*—The transformation process helps school leaders, teachers, and staff members increase their energy, determination, and persistence to ensure students succeed. There is a high intensity level to ensure students succeed.
- *Culture*—The school transformation leads to a school culture and environment that is built on trust and teamwork, all in order to ensure students succeed.
- *Connectedness*—Through the school transformation, the school's many systems become connected or aligned in an effort to ensure students succeed and are prepared for the next level.

- *Leadership*—The school's leadership no longer works in isolation, but instead, collaboratively with teachers, staff members, and other stakeholders.
- *Collective Journey*—Everyone is working together, committed to the same vision.

TRANSFORMATIVE ROLES

School Leaders:

- Model the embrace of change;
- Communicate the need for change;
- Recognize and celebrate others who embrace change;
- Help stakeholders to overcome fears of change, as well as obstacles, setbacks, and barriers.

Teachers and Staff Members:

- Embrace the change process;
- Utilize challenges, obstacles, and setbacks as opportunities for growth and learning;
- Communicate to school leaders additional steps and strategies needed for success;
- Engage students in the classroom, utilizing their input to help bring about change in the teaching and learning process, thus making learning student-centered.

RESEARCH AND TRANSFORMATION

Change is a critical component of school transformation. The entire motive behind school transformation is creating change within the school that will lead to a better learning organization for students. As mentioned earlier, school transformation is simply about students. Being about students has several different layers, but at the end of the day, the essence of being a student-centered school is about creating supports, programs, and services that will help students to succeed. School leaders, teachers, and staff members must be willing to go the extra mile to ensure all students are engaged and successful.

More importantly, all school staff must have a laser focus on ensuring students are prepared for the next level, whether that is the next grade level, college, or the workforce. Though change is needed, change will be difficult. According to Goodman and Loh (2012), as schools commit to change, they still face current pressures. As schools seek to transform to meet the demands of tomorrow, the pressures of today's schools and the growing diversity in student need only compound the complexities for school leaders, teachers, and staff members.

The pressures, obstacles, and challenges that schools will undoubtedly face are opportunities that can lead to bigger changes in the school's constructs, which are desperately needed in many of today's schools. Change should be embraced as a means to create learning experience, opportunities, and spaces that are student-centered. Additionally, change is an opportunity to improve the overall effectiveness of the school and staff, which is not necessarily a bad thing.

Communication is an essential part of the change process. According to Carter, Goldsmith, Smallwood, Sullivan, and Ulrich (2013), effective communication is key to creating effective change throughout the organization. School leaders must be able to communicate the need for change, the change process, and the goals for transformation. Just as important, school leaders must be able to describe how the change will impact teachers, staff members, students, and other stakeholder groups. Additionally, school leaders must be able to demonstrate how the transformation process will help create a better learning institution for students.

Change impacts all facets of the school, as an organization, including school leadership. Visionary leaders are willing to embrace change as a process to grow, mediocre to ineffective leaders may not be as willing to accept or embrace change as a needed component to improve the outcomes for students. According to Adserias, Charleston, and Jackson (2017), organizational change is mainly impacted by the leader.

In other words, school leaders are the gatekeepers to lasting and effective change within schools. School leaders must be aware of how much their leadership plays into the overall success of the transformation process. Ideally throughout the process and even before the transformation process begins, school leaders must share the burden of success with others. But ultimately, the principal, as the chief executive officer of the school, bears the burden and the responsibility for the success of the transformation process.

Without question, schools need to transform into educational centers that are characterized by personalization, collaboration, and empowerment. These "big rocks" will help position the school to be competitive in the future with new forms of education that are already beginning to expand across the nation. As noted by Hall and Hord (1987), for change to take place in schools, change must first be understood by stakeholders and then embraced.

Long-term change will only occur when stakeholders are committed to change and understand why change is needed. Every school needs to embrace change and continually look for opportunities to change. Students need every school leader, teacher, and staff member to be working toward creating the best learning opportunities and possibilities that will lead to their success, so that every student succeeds!

TRANSFORMATIVE POINTS TO CONSIDER

- The idea is simple. If school leaders, teachers, and staff members refuse to change, they limit their ability to meet the changing needs of today's students. Furthermore, their refusal or reluctance to change will be the nail in the coffin for public education in America.
- Sometimes, school leaders, teachers, and staff members make transformation too complicated, though without question it is difficult. The obstacle that most school administrators can't overcome is the idea of change. Educators must get to the point where change is embraced and encouraged, which would make transformation so much easier.
- Change helps the school continue to move. The school as an institution is ripe for change, if school administrators, teachers, and staff members are willing to allow change to occur. Though everyone should be involved with improving the school, school administrators are responsible for igniting the fire that starts the transformation engine.
- School leaders may lead the transformation process; they, however, do not carry the burden of change alone. School transformation, to be effective, must be a team effort.
- Without change, schools will never be able to reach the optimum level of performance that our students desperately need today. Change allows schools to really challenge their abilities to create the best learning environments that result in student success. Transformation, the actual changing ways schools are structured and operate, is more about meeting the needs of students through changing the ways schools approach the instructional process.

PRACTICAL INTRODUCTION

The purpose of school transformation is to change the school's processes, structures, culture, focus, or goals. Schools begin the transformation process usually out of necessity, as a result of test scores, school climate assessments, teacher turnover, or leadership effectiveness. No matter the reason, school transformation requires a certain level of change throughout the process. School leaders will need to clearly communicate the purpose behind the change, the reasons why change is needed.

Additionally, school leaders will need to communicate the urgency for change; in other words, why change is needed now and not down the road. The key to transformation is the ability of the school leader to engage others in the process, obtaining the support of stakeholders to embrace change as a means to improve student success and teacher and staff effectiveness. Change is eventually going to happen; would it not be better if it was initiated by school leaders, teachers, staff, and students, instead of people and groups on the outside?

At the end of the day, school transformation results in noticeable and long-term change in schools. Stakeholders need to see and feel how the transformation process has resulted in changing the school's dynamics. In some schools the level of change will require large-scale, structural, and cultural change. While in some cases, the change may be small, but noticeable, simple process transformation like master schedules or policies still require input and feedback from stakeholders and should not be the sole decision of school leaders.

For change to be effective, stakeholders must support and be committed to the change process. The process must become more relevant, rigorous, and personalized for students. Change is difficult as many school leaders, teachers, and staff members view change in terms of their role, and not how change benefits students. Not all change is good, but in most cases, change can improve, if done correctly, the overall school, including leadership performance, teacher effectiveness, organizational efficiencies, and student success.

School leaders must focus on putting change in terms of student success. Change must be seen as a process to ensure more students experience success. Also, if change is seen in terms of improving the school as an organization, teachers and staff members are more willing to embrace the change efforts. But as mentioned throughout each chapter, if stakeholders have a voice in the change process, they are more willing to embrace it.

KEY QUESTIONS

The Key Questions are meant to help school leaders begin thinking about the transformation principles in relation to their schools.

- What school components need to change in order for the school to move forward and to help students experience success?
- Why is change needed?
- How will change help to improve the school's strategic focus?
- How will change help to improve the school's overall culture?

CHANGE TRANSFORMED

Strategy: Develop a Strategic Focus

"The secret of change is to focus all of your energy, not on fighting the old, but on building the new."

—Socrates

School transformation is about change, as we continue to mention throughout each chapter. Change is often needed in schools because many of them lack a strategic focus and a long-term strategy. Many schools operate from day-to-day, barely able to keep their head above water. The only strategy in place in many schools is the short-term strategy to start and end school on predetermined dates; otherwise, there is no strategy in place.

School leaders have a responsibility to work with teachers, staff members, students, parents, guardians, and members of the community to develop a clear and concise long-term strategy that is inspiring. The school's strategic focus must be inspiring to stakeholders as a way to encourage commitment to the plan and purpose. School transformation helps to develop a common focus within the school, a long-term goal that everyone aspires to help the school reach.

Change is often needed because schools lack a clear focus. School leaders have all experienced or observed schools with no clear focus. Those schools jump from one thing to another, without ever reaching a goal or success. Many schools continue to experience struggles and failure, without ever realizing the need for change and the development of strategic focus. As a result of failing to realize the need for a clear, strategic focus, student success continues to decrease or remain stagnant, staff turnover is high, and community support for the school remains low.

Change helps the school to chart a course with a long-term strategy that is inspiring and visionary. School leaders, teachers, and staff members work together throughout the transformation process to develop a strategic focus on student success, organizational effectiveness, and improvements in the teaching and learning process. As a result of having a strategy, a blueprint to success, the school remains focused on goals even during times of uncertainty, setbacks, or challenges.

The school's strategic plan helps to ensure that the transformation process continues and change happens as a means to continue the journey. If schools do not have a clear focus, specifically on creating the best outcomes for students, then simply put, students will not be successful. It is recommended that school leaders, teachers, and staff members take the necessary time to create a strategy that will help guide the transformation process.

Strategy: Be a Collaborative Change Leader

> "A leader takes people where they want to go. A great leader takes people where they don't necessarily want to go, but ought to be."
>
> —Rosalynn Carter

Leadership is critical in all organizations. Organizations rise and fall based on the effectiveness of the person who sits in the leadership chair. Back in chapter 1, several business leaders were mentioned who were identified as effective, innovative, and mavericks (not afraid to take risks). Throughout the book, the importance of school leadership has been emphasized. Furthermore, school leaders have been encouraged to take the bull by the horns and lead the school transformation process.

There is a strong correlation between school leadership and school transformation; the successes of both are interconnected. Though teachers, staff members, and other stakeholders must be part of the transformation process, school leaders are vision critical to creating systematic change throughout schools. Yes, school leadership matters and impacts so much in and around the school.

We highlight leadership in the change principle because, going forward, leadership, in most schools, must change. Schools can no longer have organizational structures that limit decision-making to an individual or a select few. The transformation process will require a team of leaders, within the school, working together to move the school forward. Throughout the transformation process, there is a critical need for the school's leadership to be collaborative.

The need for collaborative leadership is emphasized throughout *Can Every School Succeed? Bending Constructs to Transform an American Icon*, because of the complexities that schools face going forward, including throughout the transformation process. Also, collaborative school leadership is stressed, as school leaders cannot shoulder the burden of creating sustainable change alone. In fact, the point can be made that collaboration should be part of the school's leadership fabric: all decisions should be made in the collaborative arena, not in isolation.

School leaders have an amazing opportunity to create meaningful change in the school by working with others. Additionally, school leaders have the opportunity to empower those stakeholders who are typically silent throughout the transformation process. The change process encourages all stakeholders to be school leaders in school, particularly teacher and student leaders.

The transformation process provides an excellent opportunity to empower teachers to become leaders: stepping forward to help others to embrace change, developing and communicating the school's vision for change, and engaging diverse perspectives in the decision-making process. Teacher leaders are critical in twenty-first-century schools, and not just during the transformation process. We encourage school leaders, if they have not already embraced teacher leadership, to do so immediately. Without teacher leadership, schools are truly crippled and restricted from transforming and moving forward.

Student leadership is rarely mentioned in the school transformation process, but in fact, is a critical component in changing the school's structures. The school leadership must require students to be part of transforming the school and designing schools that are student-centered and innovative. Furthermore, school leadership must create processes and the expectation that student voice is woven throughout the decision-making process.

As schools transform, school leaders must insist on student voice to be more than just survey responses. Many schools do a great job of surveying students, but rarely, engage students in the decision-making process at the individual and personal level. High-performing schools have systems and protocols where school leaders engage students directly, regularly meeting with student leaders, the student council, or one-on-one.

When students see and realize that school leaders, teachers, and staff members value their input, they attend school and become more engaged in the teaching and learning process. School leaders must help stakeholders to recognize that students and their success is at the center of the transformation process. The transformation process changes not just the school as an organization, but also the leadership in schools.

If effective, the school leadership becomes more adaptable and responsive to the changing needs in the school, from students, teachers, staff members, parents, and members of the community. School leaders can no longer be isolated; they have to become the face of the school and accessible to all stakeholders. The more school leaders engage with stakeholders, making the point to listen and to be responsive to stakeholder needs, the more likely stakeholders will embrace the transformation process and the school's vision going forward.

There are numerous effective school leaders who have paved the way to creating sustainable change in schools. School leaders are encouraged to create a list of characteristics that they feel will help improve their effectiveness and also lead to successful change in the school before beginning the transformation process. Better yet, engage stakeholders in developing areas of strength and improvement areas for the school leadership.

Seek input from stakeholders in transforming the school leadership. The transformation process and school leadership will be strengthened by engaging others in developing the overall plan for change. Diversity in ideas and different perspectives will lead to stronger and more sustainable change. Furthermore, inclusion of different viewpoints leads to stronger commitment to the transformation that is occurring in the school.

Strategy: Communicate the Vision . . . Regularly

> "For managers who believe that giving way information weakens their control, consider that sharing information is reciprocal."
>
> —The Emerson Group

One characteristic that is consistent with all effective organizational leaders is the ability to communicate. Effective school leaders understand the importance of conveying a message and painting a picture in words that all stakeholders understand. Schools need leaders who can help others to understand the transformation process, the school's vision, and ultimate goal through words.

The best way to engage others in the transformation process is effectively communicating the journey, the mission, the goals. Teachers, staff members, and other stakeholders are more likely to embrace change, if they understand change, and that begins with the school leader utilizing various forms of communication strategies and techniques. School leaders, especially at this stage, must not skimp on communicating the purpose behind the needed transformation.

The transformation process helps school leaders to become more aware of the changing needs of the school's stakeholders, including their communication needs. In the past, many school leaders have been deemed ineffective based on their ability, or the lack thereof, to communicate the school's vision, goals, and journey. In many cases, school leaders fail to recognize the stakeholders' communication preferences.

In today's schools, regular communication is essential as schools are changing at an increasingly rapid pace. Furthermore, utilizing a variety of communication strategies is a must. There are so many communication tools at the fingertips of school leaders. Due to the complexity of the school transformation process, school leaders must be able to use a variety of communication strategies to keep stakeholders informed and engaged.

School leaders in high-performing schools use a buffet of communication strategies to keep stakeholders engaged in the process, such as weekly memos, newsletters, social media, video messages, radio, newspaper, and flyers. There is a growing need for school leaders to keep people informed, and not just during the transformation process. School leaders would be wise to understand their stakeholders' communication preferences. Also, they should have "communication disciples," those individuals who understand the change process and can deliver the transformative message one-on-one to others.

We continue to stress the importance of collaboration in schools. Collaboration is yet another powerful and effective way to keep stakeholders informed about the school, the school's mission and vision, and the transformation process. As school stakeholders begin to collaborate, they begin to share and discuss information. School leaders can utilize collaboration as a means to spread the school's message, share information, and also identify gaps in their communication strategy.

School leaders must empower stakeholders to spread the school's message by engaging them in the direction of the school and regularly sharing information. Yet, the key communication strategy in schools today is transparency. Not only are stakeholders hungry for information, they also are in search of school leaders who truly practice transparency. Stakeholders are more willing to embrace and follow school leaders who are transparent, accessible, and ethical—as research validates over and over again.

School transformation will be strengthened if information is freely shared and the process is transparent. If the transformation process and information is isolated to just a handful of individuals, stakeholders will be less likely to embrace the journey and the subsequent changes. We must also stress that transparency is not just limited during the period of transformation. In fact, we argue that school leaders be transparent each day.

Concealing information, limiting decisions to a select few, or limited communication only leads to the disengagement of stakeholders in the school process. Transparency always improves the effectiveness of school leaders. School leaders practicing transparency strengthen stakeholders' trust and engagement in the school process. Transparent school leaders can have a huge positive impact on the school's culture. As Colin Powell said, leadership begins with trust. As such, school stakeholders are more likely to follow transparent school leaders, thus strengthening the transformation process.

School leaders must not be afraid to share the good, the bad, and the ugly throughout the change process. Limiting or keeping information from school stakeholders, only creates unnecessary barriers to transforming the school. Effective communication can help strengthen the school's transformation process. Too often, communication is reactive and not proactive in schools. School leaders are good at communicating a message after the fact, but rarely before.

Reactive messaging in the transformation process can hinder the overall success and actually derail the journey. School leaders must have a clear communication strategy throughout the transformation—ready to use and deploy—especially during setbacks. The more information about the transformation process can be shared from the start, the better the change within the school will be.

Strategy: Believe in Winning

"Winning isn't everything, but wanting to win is."

—Vince Lombardi

There must be a clear understanding that schools can succeed and students can succeed. Additionally, the only way schools succeed is when students succeed. School success cannot be absent student success. School leaders have a responsibility to help teachers and staff members to not only understand student success equals school success, but also to embrace and believe in the success formula.

Too often, school leaders, teachers, and staff members perceive themselves as successful, even as student success decreases or is absent. School transformation helps to ingrain the importance of student success into the school's culture and vision. School leaders have a responsibility to help teachers and staff members embrace the understanding that student success is paramount to the overall success of the school.

Through regular interaction with stakeholders and modeling the expectation that all students experience success, school leaders begin to help transform the school, stakeholder values, and the vision. Each day, school leaders, along with teacher leaders and staff leaders, must communicate the expectation that all students experience success: big or small. The key is that students experience success.

Schools must become organizations focused on winning; that is, students winning, which means students are prepared for college, a career, and for life.

Though many would argue that all schools are focused on student success, clearly there is a huge disconnect between belief and what the data shows. We have too many schools failing due to a variety of reasons, but at the end of the day, they fail because they are not focused on student success.

Schools often fail because they become victims of their own systems and processes, which they discover are not about student success but instead about appeasing adults or created out of compliance. School failure is real and for schools to transform, this must first be accepted as fact, not as fake. Too many students are unsuccessful because ultimately their schools are not successful.

There comes a time when believing in winning reaches critical mass. School leaders must help others to aspire to win. If you look at history, the past twenty years have been devastating to the winning spirit of school leaders, teachers, and staff members. Rarely are school leaders, teachers, and staff members offered praise for their dedication and success, even as student success in many schools has reached unprecedented levels.

Today's climate for public education requires school leaders, teachers, and staff members to begin believing in their own abilities to win, even as they face challenges and setbacks. If students are expected to succeed, to win, then school leaders, teachers, and staff members must first believe in their own ability to win! Success breeds success! School leaders, teachers, and staff members must be determined to ensure that all students succeed and believe in their abilities to do so.

We encourage school leaders, throughout the transformation process, to focus on creating schools that are student-centered and inspiring. Schools must become centers of inspiration, focused on ensuring student success and winning. There has never been a time like now, where student success is desperately needed. Students are depending on school leaders, teachers, and staff members to create the opportunities that will help them experience success.

The transformation process helps schools to change and focus on those important things in school, specifically student success. Students expect schools to focus on their needs and goals. Schools must develop a laser focus on providing services and supports to students that are relevant and personalized. To remain relevant, student success as measured by their preparedness for the next level—college, a career and life—must be the focus in all schools.

Schools can no longer utilize cookie-cutter approaches that focus on the masses. Students want learning programs, services, and supports that are personalized to their interests. School leaders must help teachers and staff members to realize that schools remain relevant by focusing on students as individuals. As a result, students experience success, leading to schools experiencing success.

TRANSFORMATIVE IDEAS FROM THE FIELD

Schools are complex organizations that are primed for change. Over the past several decades, as a result of local, state, and federal regulations and accountability models, schools have become quagmires of policies, systems, and protocols that have led to minimal increases in student success. Each day, school leaders, teachers, and staff members work to meet numerous compliance-based checklists, even as student interest in schools remain stagnant. As a result, more and more students are becoming disengaged, all while the morale of school staff continues to decrease. Schools must change.

School leaders must have a clear and concise change strategy that focuses on transforming the school from compliance centers to centers of inspiration. Schools can once again become places that encourage student creativity, inspiration, and innovation. Students desperately need schools to change and focus on their personalized needs. For far too long, schools have focused on cookie-cutter approaches to meeting the needs of the masses.

Now, schools must transform, changing to become centers of personalized learning, targeting the needs, goals, and aspirations of the individual student. As schools focus on each student, student engagement and success will drastically improve. At the end of the day, schools must focus on winning and that requires a laser focus on ensuring students succeed. School leaders, teachers, and staff members must realize and understand that marketing to the needs of the individual student is essential to the school's long-term success and sustainability.

Change is critical to engaging students in the learning process and ensuring that all students succeed. The key is that school leaders must model the embrace of change and communicate the need for change to teachers and staff members. Schools must embrace the opportunity to change in order to remain relevant in each student's pursuit to be college-, career- and life-ready, and globally competitive.

PRINCIPAL'S NOTE

"Change is hard at first, messy in the middle,
*and gorgeous at the end." —*Robin Sharma

3:10 p.m.
December 9
Room D1
Spring Water Elementary School

I have a sign in my office that is partially hidden from anyone's view but my own. "Shift happens." I was hired as the principal at Spring Water Elementary because I was seen as a change agent. However, an organization doesn't change because of just one person. It must be a team effort in order for change to be systemic and long lasting. In order to solidify our shift, I needed to not only talk the talk, but walk the walk.

My first order of business was to change around our staff meetings. I got rid of general faculty meetings in favor of grade-level professional learning community (PLC) meetings that focused on student achievement, data, and instruction rather than surface level information and housekeeping. General information could easily be sent in an e-mail or put in a memo in teachers' mailboxes.

Some teachers applauded this change; others did not. Some of them liked the opportunity to get together as it provided them an opportunity to push back on the administration and the district. There was a history of some teachers standing up at the one hour mark of a staff meeting and declaring that I either end the meeting immediately or agree to pay staff members for an extra hour of work. I knew that it would be much harder for teachers to walk out on their colleagues than me.

I was careful not to micromanage their PLC meetings. I wanted to capitalize on their newfound feeling of empowerment. Overseeing every aspect of their meetings would negate the work that had been done to shift the culture of the school. Instead of requiring weekly notes, I would ask if I could drop in on their meetings. I spent ten minutes in one, fifteen in another. I gave my thoughts when asked, being careful not to steer the conversation in one direction. Change must be organic in nature, not controlled or contrived.

I did give them talking points. Data became the focal point of every conversation I had with staff members. Before each PLC meeting I would ask them to look at particular students, assessments, or standards. I gave them the tools to dig deeper. We accomplished this by conducting root causes analysis and looking at the whole child. We looked at the locus of control, taking into consideration what we had no control over and what we could control.

The conversation quickly changed from talking about "those" kids to what we could do as educators to support all students. I brought in papers and articles about success stories from schools that mirrored our population. It was quickly realized that we didn't need new students, facilities, or curriculum. We needed to change our mindset.

We began to look differently at everything: assessment, attendance, grading, parent participation, discipline. . . . Instead of making excuses, we now looked at ways to do something about the results.

Another focal point of change revolved around the notion that many teachers often feel that they work in isolation. My staff was no different. Too often, teachers and students would enter classrooms, the door would close behind them, and it would only open up again at the next bell. In the past, there was a lot of secrecy and mystery as to what occurred in everyone's classroom.

I encouraged teaches to share best practices and to invite their colleges into their classrooms so they could see innovative instruction in action. Through the sharing of best practices in our newly defined PLCs, classroom doors were now open, with teachers inviting other teachers into their classrooms. Teachers talk to one another more than most people realize.

Soon, the word got out all over the district that Spring Water Elementary was doing things differently. Everyone wanted to take a peek. I was soon besieged by requests from principals to have their teachers come view classrooms and instructional practices in action. My staff loved it. Their feeling of empowerment continued to grow as teachers from around the district took note of their craft and expertise.

In the past, my teachers would have never allowed other teachers to be in their classrooms. It was a notion that was foreign to them, and one that provoked fear, anxiety, and doubt. You gain strength, courage, and confidence by every experience in which you really stop to look fear in the face. According to Eleanor Roosevelt, you are able to say to yourself, "I lived through this horror. I can take the next thing that comes along."

Once this hurdle was overcome, we were able to start working on building the leadership capacity of all staff members.

TAKEAWAY IDEAS

- School leaders must effectively communicate why change is important throughout the transformation process.
- Schools must become adaptable, ready to change as the needs of students change.
- Change is critical to the long-term sustainability of public schools in today's competitive educational market.
- School leaders must model the embrace of change, if teachers and staff members are expected to change.
- Student success is the prerequisite to school success.

Chapter Six

Capacity

Building Structures for New Forms of Leadership

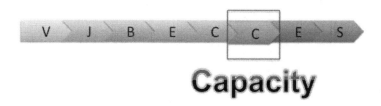

Throughout the transformation process, school leaders will be challenged by their own abilities and the abilities of others. To be clear, the transformation process should challenge school leaders to expand their vision, as they try to help the school move to a new level of performance for students. Francois de La Rouchefoucauld speaks to the fact that we must not limit opportunity to do, or become, something great for students.

From the beginning the transformation process should be pushing the school, challenging the school's ability. If change isn't challenging then the school is not trying to reach levels necessary to help the school meet the needs of the students. School leaders, teachers, and staff members must not restrict the possibilities of transforming the school, by only limiting the change process to their own zones of comfort and abilities.

School leaders, teachers, and staff members strive to push the limits and change the school in ways that will result in a better learning environment for students and better learning outcomes for students. There is an inherent need for school leaders to focus on growing the capacity to begin the transformation process in schools. Without the capacity to initiate and to lead change, the results will be less than stellar; in fact, they could cause irreparable harm to the school.

The capacity to create long-term change in schools requires school leaders, teachers, and staff members to have a growth mindset, embracing the opportunity that transforming the school can lead to many opportunities for students. Without the capacity to transform, to change, the immediate results will not be rewarding for students, nor will change be sustainable going forward.

TRANSFORMATION CORE IDEA

School transformation requires the capacity to change. The capacity to change for students involves ongoing professional learning that targets strategic change and doing what is best for students.

> For change to be effective, school leaders, teachers, and staff members must have the capacity to carry out the change process. School transformation is not easy; therefore, there will need to be a strategic plan and up front work performed in order for change to be effective and targeted. The burden of change success does not and must not fall solely on the shoulders of school leaders, but must be a collaborative effort. Transformation will require that stakeholders be provided ongoing training opportunities that will assist in ensuring the change process is consistent with the school's vision and the needs of students, leaders, and staff.

TRANSFORMATIVE KEY UNDERSTANDINGS

- *Targeted Training*—Professional learning is strategic; provide school leaders, teachers, and staff members with professional learning that is focused on helping students succeed, and understanding, embracing, and leading change.
- *Systems*—There is a school-wide system that is geared toward ensuring that processes and procedures are in place that allow transformation to occur.
- *Leading and Serving*—Leadership transforms from reacting to situations to serving stakeholders and being proactive with decisions.
- *Simplicity*—To ensure that capacity exists, change is kept simple, but transformative. Simple helps others to buy-in and commit to the process.
- *Community*—For the school to have the capacity to transform, the community has to be involved in the school process. School leaders, teachers, and staff members must look for ways to engage community and allow them to have a voice in the change.

- *Challenge*—Schools must embrace challenges as opportunities to transform in order for transformation to occur. Transformation is change that has many challenges, and schools must have the capacity to overcome those challenges.

TRANSFORMATIVE ROLES

School Leaders:

- Identify areas for growth and improvement pertaining to change;
- Identify and schedule professional learning opportunities to help grow the capacity for the transformation process;
- Establish a need for a strategic plan focused on increasing the capacity to transform;
- Maintain a sense of urgency to change and the capacity to grow.

Teachers and Staff Members:

- Self-evaluate talents and skills, identifying gaps that will need to be addressed to have the capacity for the transformation process;
- Participate in ongoing professional learning focused on transformation and leading;
- Ensure needs of students are considered;
- Be willing to admit mistakes and the need for assistance.

RESEARCH AND TRANSFORMATION

When school leaders decide, collectively with stakeholders, to begin the transformation process, they must understand underlying requirements. From the beginning school leaders must be developing the capacity within the organization to transform. Though many schools need to transform, often, neither school leaders nor stakeholders have the capacity to lead the change necessary to result in positive outcomes for students.

But, as Sigurðardóttir and Sigþórsson (2015) found, school improvement can occur, and the capacity to lead can form within schools. The key to both is the willingness to accept and embrace continuous improvement. Within the school transformation capacity is not always an indication that change can occur. In many cases, school leaders must have the capacity to realize that change is needed and the capacity to communicate, launch, and evaluate the change process effectively.

Often, school leaders, teachers, and staff members begin the transformation without having the capacity to fully implement change, much less carry through over the long-term. According to Feeney (2009), most school leaders do not have the capacity to lead the change process in schools. As we continue to mention throughout this book, transformation can be complicated and daunting for many school leaders.

School leaders should take the time to investigate the transformation process and when possible visit other schools that have gone through a strategic school improvement process. By networking with other school leaders who have successfully implemented change protocols or transformed the school from an adult-centered institution to a student-centered institution, school leaders will be able to access the supports and services needed to help create the change needed in their schools.

As experienced school leaders, we also realize that at this point many will ask: what exactly are the characteristics of capacity required for a transformative school leader? According to Chuang (2013), the essential skills needed to possess the capacity to lead a dynamic organization, such as a 21st century learning institution, are: 1) develop self-awareness; 2) understand cultural stereotypes; 3) increase self-assurance; 4) look at the bigger picture; 5) create a vision and be able to sell it; 6) develop a global mindset; 7) gain and offer supports; 8) develop effective communication skills; 9) search for and utilize available resources; 10) create appropriate motivational techniques; and 11) take social responsibility seriously. The skills Chuang identified are valuable skills that when developed and acquired by school leaders, can transform the school and allow for change to be sustained into the future. Furthermore, according to King and Bouchard (2011), schools must be flexible and have the necessary supports needed to grow the capacity needed. This requires that school leaders think strategically and seek opportunities to make decisions through collaboration instead of in isolation.

These are important characteristics that we also believe define capacity in terms of transforming schools. We also think empowerment is a needed skill. Based on our experience we feel that without the empowerment of others throughout the transformation process, the school simply does not have the capacity to change. As mentioned previously transformation is simply too complex to be the responsibility of one individual in schools.

Growing the capacity to initiate and to lead school transformation will take a team approach. The time of traditional organizational structures in schools, where leadership is isolated to the school's principal or administrative team, is over. The capacity to change, in fact, to lead, comes with experience and the willingness to grow. School leaders must be leaders who embrace the growth process as a means to develop the capacity to commit to change within schools.

TRANSFORMATIVE POINTS TO CONSIDER

- Many will discover throughout the transformation process the importance of having the capacity to lead the change. By embracing the change process, school leaders will be able to acquire the skills necessary to lead others—in other words, their capacity as a twenty-first-century school leader will grow exponentially.
- The capacity to lead change is a roadblock for many school administrators. They either fail to understand the transformation process or lack the ability to lead change. The result for both is the same: change is derailed, and future efforts to improve are greatly wounded. Prior to beginning the transformation process, school administrators should assess whether or not they as leaders are ready, as well as if the school is ready for change. If not, go back to the beginning—though it may take longer, it will help the school in the long run.
- Many would argue that no leader has all of the tools and experiences necessary to lead the change process in schools. However, if they are willing to embrace change and effectively execute it, capacity is enhanced to become transformative school leaders.
- Capacity to transform schools must be understood. A school leader's capacity to lead and create change is vital to the school's willingness to begin change. When a school administrator has the capacity to lead change, this means that he or she can first clearly communicate why change is needed and in the end also celebrate and recognize when change occurs. Capacity isn't always about the Xs and Os in the transformation playbook, it also includes often overlooked or undervalued tools, such as communication and celebration. Teachers, staff members, and even parents will embrace school leaders who have the capacity to communicate the path to school transformation that they are ready to begin and also have a sense of humor even when confronted with barriers.

PRACTICAL INTRODUCTION

The capacity to lead transformation is often overlooked by many practitioners. The capacity to begin the transformation process is the responsibility of not only school leaders, but teachers and staff. The key is to engage others in the process from the beginning, enlisting teachers and staff who embrace change, are willing to take risks, and are innovative in their classrooms or current roles.

School leaders need to grow an army of stakeholders who can help begin this important process, by providing opportunities to collaborate, attend training, visit schools that have been transformed, and be part of the decision-making process from the beginning. School leaders need to enlist teachers and staff members who have the experiences, willingness, abilities, and determination to make the transformation process effective.

Capacity to lead the change process is vision critical. School leaders must recognize that they must seek out opportunities that will provide them not only with the skills, experiences, and understanding to effectively lead the school transformation, but also teachers and staff members. Capacity often is used too freely in organizations as a means to communicate leadership ability.

However, with school transformation, capacity is at the heart of determining success and failure. Closely aligned with sustainability, capacity ensures the ability to implement and evaluate transformative processes to ensure alignment to the school's vision, goals, and the needs of students. School leaders, along with teachers and staff members must exhibit leadership—leading the change—above all else.

KEY QUESTIONS

The Key Questions are meant to help school leaders begin thinking about the transformation principles in relation to their schools.

- As you begin the transformation process, what are the school's goals for change? How will students benefit? How will the transformation improve the school?
- How does your school's plan for transformation push school leaders, teachers, and staff members outside of their zones of comfort?
- How do you know your school has the capacity to change? What skills do school leaders, teachers, and staff members have that will help lead change in school?
- What processes and strategies are in place that will help school leaders, teachers, and staff members learn and acquire the skills and capacity to help transform the school?

CAPACITY TRANSFORMED

Strategy: Diversify Leadership

"Diversity is the engine of invention. It generates creativity that enriches the world."

—Justin Trudeau, Prime Minister of Canada

School transformation is a complex and in some cases a very lengthy process. Though school leaders are critical players in the transformation process, they cannot and should not shoulder the entire burden of changing the school. In fact, for the school to have the capacity to change, there must be others involved the process. Moreover, teachers and staff members must be leaders in the transformation process.

A key component of transformative leadership is diversity based on collaboration, shared decision-making, and structures that allow flexibility in the school leadership. School leaders must find ways that they can help teachers and staff members build the confidence and experience needed to be transformative leaders. Think about experiences and opportunities within the school and outside of school that can help grow the confidence needed for teachers and staff members to be effective leaders.

In many cases, visionary and transformative leaders create opportunities whereby teachers and staff members develop the skills necessary to be leaders in the school. Faculty and staff members can gain valuable knowledge and expertise by leading professional learning communities, being part of the school's leadership team that is tasked with making school-wide decisions, acting as mentors and coaches to other teachers and staff, and working closely with the school administration in leading day-to-day operations.

If opportunities do not exist for collaborative leadership in schools, school leaders must find ways to create opportunities for others to be part of leading the school. There can never be enough leaders waiting on the bench. Top organizations develop strong leaders as a means to have a clear succession plan in place should a vacancy occur at the top and help carry out the organization's vision.

Schools are like many businesses and corporations. There needs to be a strong bench of leaders waiting in the wings should there be a vacancy at the top. As mentioned earlier, school transformation is often derailed by school leaders leaving in midstream or near the end of the transformation process. School transformation is most effective when there are leaders in the background who understand the transformation components and goals and are committed to the school's vision, who can step in and continue the transformation process.

There should be a seamless transition where the transformation continues and even becomes stronger should a vacancy occur. Continued change only happens when teachers and staff members are empowered to be leaders throughout the transformation process. Also, by including others in the decision-making process, leaders are more suited to communicate the school's vision for transformation, which strengthens empowering others to be leaders throughout the process.

Teachers and staff members must be prepared to step into roles that will challenge their ability to be leaders, while also encouraging them to use their skills to ensure the transformation is effective. Growing others to be leaders also strengthens the school's capacity. School leaders must not give up on involving others in the transformation process and empowering them to be leaders throughout the process. As school leaders, we must put ourselves in the shoes of teachers and staff members and come to identify key opportunities and experiences that will help garner the support of others and their subsequent step to becoming leaders.

The capacity to lead transformation is based on the willingness of school leaders to recognize the need for others to be leaders throughout the process. Additionally, the school's ability to transform will be determined by the school leader's ability to help others to become visionary leaders. Additionally, the school leader's ability to inspire others to be leaders will be critical to the growth of others to be leaders in the school.

The school leader can increase the willingness of others to serve as leaders by publicly acknowledging others when they lead in schools. Furthermore, they recognize teachers and staff members who are leaders in school by sharing more leadership authority with stakeholders and allowing others to see their support of shared decision-making. Highly effective school leaders see strength in growing leadership capacity in the school by empowering others to be leaders.

Strategy: Commit to Change and Success

"Good teams are committed to the team's mission and to each other personally. Good leaders inspire and build this commitment and trust."

—Lee Ellis

The need for visionary leaders throughout the transformation process is indeed a critical component to growing leadership capacity in schools. School leaders need to be committed to and believe in the change process. The commitment of school leaders can help move the transformation needle considerably, as they are more involved in the process; more willing to take more strategic risks; embrace change and innovation; and exhibit energy, determination, and persistence, even during challenges, obstacles, and setbacks.

The capacity to lead change requires that school leaders be completely committed to school transformation and willing to go the extra mile to ensure success. Likewise, the capacity to lead change requires school leaders understand the need to engage others in leading the transformation process, which can help grow the commitment of others to the change process. Commitment is a precursor to capacity. Without commitment, a school cannot have the capacity to change.

School transformation in many cases is a lengthy process, as overnight successes are rare or next to nonexistent. As a result, successful transformation requires school leaders who can go the length of the process. Additionally, school leaders need the tenacity and willingness to push through the many roadblocks and setbacks that they will almost certainly experience. Their ability to overcome challenges and setbacks will prove to be helpful to teachers and staff members, as they too will need to overcome similar problems and setbacks.

School leaders will not be able rush the process to grow capacity within schools. Furthermore, growing capacity is a continual process that school leaders must constantly visit, just as the transformation process is a continual process. School leaders also must be committed not only to the transformation process, but to ensuring all students experience success as a result of the implemented changes.

The school leadership's commitment to student success is needed just as much as, if not more than, a commitment to the transformation process. Ultimately the change process is about creating changes that will result in students experiencing success and becoming prepared for the next level. So really you could say that the commitment to student success is far more important. As mentioned previously, the urgency for change is at its all-time high, which is based on the urgency to make sure that all students are achieving.

The commitment to transforming also requires that school leaders commit to ensuring that teachers and staff members have the resources and supports necessary to change. Too often, school leaders expect teachers and staff to change openly and willingly, without ever realizing that some basic resources and supports are needed for change to occur. The biggest support necessary is that teachers and staff members must have the support from school leaders.

School leaders must assure stakeholders that change is good and if it fails that they will take full responsibility. Teachers and staff members often indicate the fear of failure as an obstacle that prevents change from happening. School transformation can be perceived as risky with many uncertainties. School leaders can help teachers and staff members to move the needle by taking the fear of failure away. School leaders need teachers and staff members to focus on student success and creating the best learning opportunities for students.

The capacity to lead will take school leaders who are visionary and goal oriented; those who are committed, wholeheartedly, to the purpose of transformation. Transformation is not for the faint of heart and will test the resolve of school leaders, which is why commitment cannot be understated or underestimated. The more committed school leaders are to transforming school structures, starting first with embracing change themselves, the better the change process will be for the school and stakeholders.

Change starts with school leaders who are committed to change that will result in the best outcomes for students. The commitment of school leaders, teachers, and staff members will be tested throughout the change process. Remain focused on why change is needed: to create the best learning environment and opportunities for students. Look for opportunities that will result in others being part of the transformation process to grow the capacity to change and lead in others, which only strengthens a school's ability to transform.

Strategy: Encourage Collaboration

"Alone we are smart. Together we are brilliant."

—Steven Anderson, Educator

School transformation is often viewed as a one person show. That is, school transformation must start and end with the school leadership; they alone carry the burden of change within the school. This mindset is the result of decades of school leadership structures all leading to the principal's desk. For transformation to be effective there must be a culture of collaboration, which will help lead to leadership capacity in the school.

Rigid and narrow organizational structures may have worked previously, but to transform public education, centralized leadership structures will no longer be effective or useful, as schools are changing rapidly. The speed of change that is occurring in schools, largely as a result of an aging teacher and staff workforce and diversifying student body, will require school leaders, teachers, and staff members all to be leaders in schools.

School leaders must embrace the concept of collaboration as a means to transform the school. There are too many "bells and whistles" for school leaders to attempt to transform the school alone. Frankly, the idea that a school leader could make the change needed alone is just unrealistic. Collaboration is a requirement in the transformation process, as it leads to capacity to lead in schools. There is no better way to grow a bench full of leaders in a school than creating a culture of collaboration.

The school must have an emphasis on collaboration. School leaders, working closely with teachers and staff members must identify obstacles and barriers that prevent collaboration from occurring. Those obstacles and barriers that prevent collaboration from happening are probably the same obstacles and barriers that will work against change within the school.

The quickest way to remove obstacles and barriers to collaboration is to ask teachers and staff members to identify them. Time and opportunity are the two most mentioned obstacles or barriers to collaboration based on our experience as school leaders. Time and opportunity will also plague the transformation process. Beware: people will always say that they do not have the time to change or have the opportunity to change due to paperwork, meetings, and workload.

School leaders must find ways to help teachers and staff members find new roads around the obstacles and barriers so that change and collaboration can occur. There are so many opportunities for collaboration to exist; we need to take the time to see them. Though time is valuable, there is ample time to collaborate and push the limits to transform the school.

We have to prioritize collaboration as a means to improve and change the teaching and learning processes. There will be no better time to transform the school and create a lasting impact on student success and the effectiveness of the school. It takes very little time to collaborate, and school leaders must make collaboration a priority throughout the transformation process as a means to grow the capacity to lead within the school.

Strategy: Create Flexible Leadership Structures

"Stay committed to your decisions, but stay flexible in your approach."

—Tony Robbins

Schools have become victims of a very rigid system with little flexibility. Transformation is about changing the traditional structures that have formed so that the teaching and learning process is more tailored to the goals and needs of students. Additionally, transformation works to restore autonomy and flexibility throughout the teaching and learning process in schools.

Schools often find themselves restricted, helpless in many cases, to meet the needs of students. Furthermore, simple, outdated processes, rules, and a lack of vision often hinder the teaching and learning process. As such, the capacity to transform is also impacted, restricted, and even prevented from occurring due to the school's structures. The structures that can help lead to the capacity to transform and to lead in schools can vary from school to school.

Overall the structures that typically impact school transformation and leadership are the school's organizational structures, professional learning communities, policies, and procedures, as well as the school's strategic plan. There are many more, but for the most part, these are the major structures that can either help or restrict the transformation process. For capacity to form, school leaders must work closely with teachers and staff members to improve the structures.

School structures must become responsive to the needs of the students, teachers, staff members, school leaders, and the school as a whole. Too often, schools, and in particular school leaders, allow structures to confine decision-making to predetermined processes and protocols. Countless outdated structures are counterproductive to capacity building in schools and prevent change from occurring.

As experienced school leaders, we recognize the importance of structures in schools; however, we also have a belief that schools need the flexibility to meet the diverse challenges that confront all schools today. Leadership capacity cannot form if the school's structures are too rigid. Schools, like other organizations, need the flexibility to adapt. Most traditional structures found in schools overlook the importance of shared decision-making, stakeholder empowerment as leaders, collaboration, and sustainability.

In most cases, school structures and protocols are designed to address the now, not the future. Many of the structures fall short in dealing with the long-term strategic needs of the school. In many cases, rigidity results in the school lacking a bench of leaders, low student engagement due to outdated instructional programming, low teacher morale, and high teacher and staff turnover.

TRANSFORMATIVE IDEAS FROM THE FIELD

School leaders are the chief executive officers (CEOs) of the school—or at least they should be. With others, working as a team, they help to set the school's vision for the long-term and for the transformation process. As the CEO, the school leader, to effectively lead and manage the school, must empower others to be leaders, which helps grow the capacity to lead the transformation process.

To successfully transform, school leaders, as well as others, must have the vision and capacity for transformation. If a school leader has never successfully transformed a school, directly or indirectly as a member of the team, they will probably struggle throughout the process and possibly even fail. Look to create a team approach to transforming the school and view transformation as a school-wide opportunity to grow the capacity to change.

Novice school leaders should not be discouraged from beginning the transformation process. In fact, they should begin and work closely with veteran transformative leaders and seek assistance from others such as teachers and staff members. Not only should they seek assistance from teachers and staff members, they should also empower them to be change agents and leaders in the school.

High levels of collaboration can help lead to developing a collective capacity to change the school. Collaboration also helps others to embrace change, as they are part of the decision-making process and actively creating a school that is better for students. Without question, schools need to change. Too many schools are still operating under outdated modes of learning that will ultimately come nowhere close to meeting the changing demands of our students.

Today's students, no matter what school they attend, have the desire and expectation to be competitive. No student wants to fail, contrary to what many believe. Students become disengaged for several reasons, but largely as a result of outdated modes of learning that fail to meet the needs and goals of our students. Schools must have the capacity to change if students are expected to be prepared for college, a career, and life.

PRINCIPAL'S NOTES

"The most valuable of all capital is that invested in human beings." —Alfred Marshall

8:15 a.m.
January 25
Morning Supervision—Front Parking Lot
Spring Water Elementary School

Our school was in the middle of a renaissance. There was electricity in the air that had been missing at the school for quite some time. Teachers were happy, parents were happy. Most importantly, our students were happy. They were learning from teachers who were once again excited about teaching. When I arrived at Spring Water Elementary, getting teachers to participate in professional development was like pulling teeth.

Now, they sought it out on their own. I was bombarded with requests to participate in conferences, workshops, and lectures. Most of these requests happened before school as I supervised the front parking lot, chatting with parents and greeting students. I said "yes" to all of them. How could I say no when I was being asked in front of parents? I also understood that parents liked to hear about their children's teachers attending conferences and keeping up with current instructional trends.

I did make one request.

I promised to send them to their conference or workshop, but they needed to come back and present what they had learned to the rest of the staff. Agreements were made, travel arrangements were solidified, and conference fees were paid. Upon their return, I debriefed with them, as I was also eager to learn what they had discovered. I informed the staff that instead of their regular professional learning community (PLC) meeting the following week, they would attend a professional development session put on by one of their colleagues.

We now had experts in our own ranks. I started to get requests from teachers and principals at other schools to send our teacher experts over to them to deliver professional development. Additionally, teachers from other schools were sent over to us to observe our teachers. Pretty soon, the district came calling and requested that our teachers present at the next district professional development sessions, which occurred every trimester.

My teachers were beaming. Again, there was an electricity in the air that was unmistakable.

Teachers at Spring Water Elementary School were seen as teacher leaders in the areas of technology, project-based learning, STEM, cross-curricular instruction, and student-centered instruction. They believed in themselves more than ever. Their confidence was invigorating. This led to one of our greatest achievements.

Risk-taking.

My teachers had told me that in the past, they were discouraged from taking instructional and program risks. They were told to always stick with the given curriculum and not to stray too far from what had always been done at the school. I posted the following quote on my office white board and let it marinate with staff who came in and out of my office:

> The most dangerous phrase in the language is, "We've always done it this way." —Grace Hopper.

It was vital that we took risks and tried new things.

I knew I had to lead by example, so I tried out a few ideas I had gotten from other principals at other schools. Some of the ideas translated well to our school and population. Other ideas were colossal failures, which I had to embrace and own. I didn't mind the failures as they allowed my staff to see that it was alright to go out on a limb and make a mistake.

Little by little, they stepped out of their comfort zone. Just as with me, some of their ideas worked, others did not. No judgments were made and no one was left out to dry. I am confident that the staff would not have tried out these new ideas the year before. Their newfound empowerment and confidence was allowing them to become better, more innovative teacher leaders. My investment in them had paid off. We had built capacity in the staff. Now we had to put it all together and execute our vision in its entirety.

TAKEAWAY IDEAS

- School leaders must evaluate their capacity to lead the transformation and the overall preparedness of the school to change prior to beginning the transformation process.
- School transformation is too complex to limit leadership to one single individual.
- The capacity to lead change will take a bench full of leaders, ready to lead when the opportunity arises throughout the transformative process.
- Capacity to lead the transformation in schools requires structures that are adaptable to the changing diverse needs of students, teachers, staff members, and the school.

Chapter Seven

Execution

Implementing the Strategy

At some point along the transformative journey, the vision for change must be effectively and strategically executed. School leaders, teachers, and staff members can have the best vision on paper, but if they fail to align processes to ensure effective execution of the strategy, success will not occur. There must a clear and concise plan to ensure that the strategy for change is expertly executed as communicated and as needed.

In most cases, school leaders will have a short window to begin the transformation process; therefore, they need to make sure that they have a well-communicated and team-developed strategy. Having a strategy that will help to execute the change process will help schools overcome the obstacles, challenges, and setbacks that will occur. Change is needed in schools, as validated by leading school researchers. As evident by daily news stories, many schools are struggling to understand the current societal demands of public education, specifically, understanding twenty-first-century students.

As pressures for schools to meet the changing and increasing demands of our students continue to increase, schools must begin to develop a long-term strategic transformative plan that is aligned to the needs of students. Executing the strategic plan is the only way the school will fulfill the requirements established by the school's vision. According to Morris Change, former CEO of the Taiwan Semiconductor Manufacturing Company, "Without strategy, execution is aimless. Without execution, strategy is useless" (Yohn, 2012).

The school may have an excellent vision that is student focused; however, without a strategy or plan, the vision is just a dream. At some point the school will ultimately have to implement a plan; the key, however, is to make sure that time is spent prior to beginning the transformation process. If schools fail to create a plan and clearly identify components, responsibilities, and targets, then the school will likely end up at a less appealing point. Transformation does not happen by coincidence, but through strategic decisions and a strategic plan that can be effectively executed.

TRANSFORMATION CORE IDEA

School transformation must help to *execute* the overall strategic plan and school's vision. Execution of the strategic plan and the change process is essential to helping students succeed and become prepared for the next level.

> The purpose and need for change must be closely aligned to the school's vision. In order to execute the deliverable of the school's strategic goals and student academic targets, the execution of the transformation process must be spot on. School leaders must model risk-taking throughout the process. They must be willing to push the boundaries of the school's teaching and learning program, as well as other organizational components and structures. No area of the school's instructional program or operations is too sacred not to be evaluated for transformation. School leaders, along with teachers and staff members, must embrace the change opportunity as a means to provide students the best learning program and environment that will lead to their success. Executing a well-developed transformation plan takes careful consideration of students' needs, goals, and aspirations.

TRANSFORMATIVE KEY UNDERSTANDINGS

- *Priority*—School leaders must execute the transformation priorities. The priorities must be strategic and target creating the best learning organization and environment that will ensure student success and preparedness for the next level.
- *The Mission*—Execute the mission to change the teaching and learning process to be personalized, rigorous, engaging, and innovative.
- *Communication*—Communication will be mission critical as school leaders, teachers, and staff members begin to execute the transformation process.
- *Inspiration*—School leaders must be inspiring, constantly challenging stakeholders to embrace the opportunity to create lasting change for stu-

dents, as well as striving to reach new, higher levels. School leaders need to be inspiring, especially when obstacles, setbacks, and barriers form.

- *Allocate Resources and Supports*—School leaders ensure that resources and supports are allocated to ensure that the transformation is successful. Furthermore, the resources and supports are allocated to support student success and preparedness.
- *Team Strategies*—School leaders work to ensure that teachers, staff members, students, parents and guardians, and members of the community can offer strategies that will lead to improvements throughout the transformation. Transformation requires a collective execution.
- *Celebrations*—School leaders, teachers, and staff members will need to celebrate early wins, no matter the size or impact. Celebrations help to continue progress and to help stakeholders to remain focused on the larger goals, not the obstacles or setbacks.

TRANSFORMATIVE ROLES

School Leaders:

- Lead the transformation process;
- Take risks and encourage others to push the boundaries of the teaching and learning process;
- Communicate progress, accomplishments, and setbacks;
- Identify next steps in the transformation process;
- Measure stakeholder engagement and support of the transformation process periodically.

Teachers and Staff Members:

- Act with urgency and purpose;
- Implement components of the transformation process;
- Ensure that the process is meeting the needs of students;
- Continue to push ahead even when faced with setbacks, challenges, and obstacles.

RESEARCH AND TRANSFORMATION

The execution of the plan is an obstacle that typically derails the transformation process. Typically, school leaders follow the steps in the transformation process only to fail when the plan is executed. The failure that many schools experience is not the failure of deciding to change, but executing the process. School leaders approach the crucial step where the plan is implemented, only to fail. According to Fogg (1999), the talk of change is cheap, as talk is not going to make change happen.

For change to occur, school leaders must step up to the plate and ensure the change process is being implemented successfully. Moving transformation from an idea into actual practice requires school leaders who are visionary and organized. According to Steel and Young (1991), implementing a strategic plan requires effective management skills. School leaders at this stage of the transformation process will need to have skills that will result in executing the transformation plan precisely, while adapting the plan to address changes in the school environment, stakeholder needs, and obstacles or barriers.

The school leader cannot just say go, as the transformation process is not a race. School transformation is a strategic and complex process that requires school leader involvement, leadership, and commitment throughout the process. Additionally, though there is an urgent need for change to occur in schools, the transformation should not be rushed. If the transformation is to be actually executed in schools, quality over speed must be emphasized. Implementing the transformation process will be challenging.

According to Wheeland (2003), change will require commitment. No matter how difficult executing the change is, school leaders will need to be committed to the overall process. Just as important, school leaders must build the commitment of others to the change process. The transformation process cannot be executed successfully by the school leader, but in fact, requires all stakeholders to be empowered to lead change, as we have mentioned several times throughout previous chapters.

The complexities of the transformation process only increase when school leaders attempt to create change in isolation. In fact, executing the plan will not occur successfully if the school leader limits the involvement of others. According to Nutt (1989), strategic organizations are effective by involving those who will benefit from the plan, be leaders of the plan, and help design the plan. The more school leaders are willing to empower and engage others in carrying out the change process, the more likely the plan for change will be executed. School leaders as they begin to execute the transformation will need to think like their stakeholders.

All stakeholders throughout the change process, as we mentioned previously, want to know how the change will impact them personally. For this reason, the execution of the transformation plan can be improved by helping stakeholders visualize the process. According to Nelson (2009), configuring the plan into a step-by-step process that can be seen and be touched, helps to stakeholders to commit and embrace the idea and principles of change. Stakeholder buy-in and commitment to change will assist in executing the transformation of today's schools.

TRANSFORMATIVE POINTS TO CONSIDER

- Schools, and ultimately students, need school administrators who can execute change. Schools need school administrators who are more than just talk, as leaders have spoken about and discussed change long enough.
- Execution of the plan is always the most difficult process. School administrators must persist no matter the situation and help others realize that they too are responsible for ensuring change occurs.
- Why does school transformation seem to rarely succeed? It is because school leaders fail to have a clear, executable plan for change. Schools are faced with increasing pressures to achieve; therefore, school administrators try to rush the process without having a strategy.
- Executing the school's plan for transformation requires school administrators who favor collaboration and shared decision-making. Transformation is only successful when the goals are shared among all stakeholders. Collaboration is a critical component during the strategy phase, as no one person should develop the plan for the school. Developing the strategic framework in isolation will hinder the success of the school transformation process.

PRACTICAL INTRODUCTION

School transformation is all about change and that requires execution. Execution means that school leaders, teachers, and staff members have ensured that: (1) the school's vision and vision for transformation are aligned; (2) the goals of transformation have a laser focus on student success and instructional effectiveness; (3) the school structures are conducive to collaborative leadership and shared decision-making; and (4) the transformation is sustainable. School leaders must work closely with stakeholders to ensure that a clear and simple blueprint is developed, identifying each step of the process and the importance of the step to the overall vision.

School leaders want others to be part of developing the school's plan for change, as creating school-wide transformation is too complex for one individual. Though school leaders may be highly effective, creating long-term sustainable change will be challenging and require a team approach to ensure success. School leaders must keep in mind why transformation is needed in schools: student success.

Today's students are increasingly diverse with a variety of needs, goals, and aspirations. As such, traditional forms of education will no longer be a viable option. Through the change process, schools transform teaching and learning to become more relevant, rigorous, and personalized for students. Students need educators to strategically execute the transformation with almost surgical precision. If schools begin the transformation process they need to follow through and give change an opportunity to work, even as challenges will occur from time to time.

KEY QUESTIONS

The Key Questions are meant to help school leaders begin thinking about the transformation principles in relation to their schools.

- How has the vision for transformation been communicated in terms of helping to execute the school's vision?
- How will the execution of the school's transformation strategy and vision be evaluated and monitored?
- How have stakeholders been assigned roles aligned to executing the school's transformative strategy?
- What are the major execution components in your transformation strategy? Those big rocks that are critical to the school's change.
- What would you consider to be your school's surface and subsurface components? Those structures that are visible and invisible that need to be transformed?

EXECUTION TRANSFORMED

Strategy: Embrace the Vision and the Call

"Successful leaders create change not by the strength of their opinions but by inspiring others to embrace a vision of the future."

—Nick Fewings

A standard component found in all effective organizations is a vision that inspires others to be greater than what they are currently. Each employee of the organization from custodians to the receptionist to the chief executive officer is all working to become better than they were the day before. Each stakeholder realizes his or her importance to the organization achieving its goals. They are not afraid to stretch their limits, skills, or talents as they realize they are working toward something bigger than themselves. Schools today need visionary leaders at every level.

As mentioned throughout previous chapters, leadership must be shared and collaborative. Shared and collaborative leadership isn't just about empowering stakeholders to be leaders; it is about creating sustainable, visionary leadership in the school. To meet the increasing expectations and growing needs of students, school leaders, teachers, and staff members will ultimately need to work and lead together.

There is nothing that says that students can't be part of helping to design and execute the transformation plan. In fact, student voice and student leadership can actually strengthen the transformation process as schools are changing, hopefully to create better learning opportunities and environments for students. In fact, for schools to remain competitive and relevant, they must engage students in the teaching and learning process now more than ever before. Executing the school's vision is not going to be easy, but can be made easier, through shared, collaborative leadership.

Schools face an unprecedented level of pressure to perform and conform. Schools must meet what sometimes are unrealistic benchmarks that at the end of the day probably are not in line with student aspirations; yet, they are required by law to measure success by test scores. Today's school leaders must help teachers and staff members to look past current pressures and aspire to create learning environments that measure success by helping students meet their college, career, and life goals.

School leaders today must have a vision for their schools that challenge stakeholders to think about education regarding student relevance. School leaders must not be afraid to ask the question, are schools helping students to meet their goals? If not, why? If so, how? The school's vision should always challenge school leaders, teachers, and staff members to take one additional step, never settling for average.

Inspiring schools, those schools with student-centered visions, never stop pushing the limits of success, innovation, and creativity. School leaders must encourage a culture of innovation, collaboration, and shared decision-making as a means to move student success to the next level, which will move the school to the next level. There is an inherent bond between student success and school success that will never be broken. Schools must become adaptable organizations focused on meeting the diverse needs of students.

The execution of the school's vision and long-term strategy will require school leaders that are committed and visionary. Transforming a school is not for the faint of heart. There will be setbacks, barriers, and challenges that will test even the most effective and veteran school leader. The key is for school leaders to remain committed to the school's vision. Teachers and staff members, just like students, will need school leaders to model the way throughout the transformative journey.

Today's schools need the ability to move and adapt quickly to the growing demands of students. Furthermore, the ability to adapt helps the school to continue to change. Though many schools today are made from brick and mortar, the school's vision must have the flexibility to change as the needs of students change. The school's vision must grow as the needs of the students change. There are no limits to what schools can become if "change" is part of the school's DNA, which starts with a visionary and transformative school leader. Effective execution of any plan or vision will always require visionary school leadership!

Strategy: Recognize People's Contributions to the Process

> "Leaders should influence others in such a way that it builds people up, encourages and educates them so they can duplicate this attitude in others."
>
> —Bob Goshen

From time to time throughout the transformation process, setbacks, barriers, and challenges will occur. Up to this point, we have been reluctant to use the word failure. Based on our experience, failure is a mindset. Effective leaders view failure as opportunities to grow, to become bigger, better, and stronger. Visionary school leaders help others not to fear failure, but instead to embrace it as a learning opportunity.

The key to keeping the school moving forward and be a hub for change is transformative leaders who praise stakeholders even when they experience challenges. Our experience as school leaders reminds us that stakeholders need words of encouragement, as most doubt their abilities or are scared of failing. The transformation process is full of opportunities to struggle, to fall backward, or to stop.

School leaders will need to be cheerleaders who are not afraid to lend a hand to pick teachers or staff members up off the ground when they experience a setback. When the school faces an abyss, a quagmire of decades-laid plans-and-processes, school leaders must be the people in the room that turns the light on and shows the way forward. From time to time, the transformative process may seem impossible; continue to press forward, if only for curiosity's sake.

Students are depending on school leaders, teachers, and staff members to change schools so that they are more open, flexible, and geared toward their interests. Transformative leaders understand that relationships are also critical to offering praise. School leaders must build relationships with teachers and staff members that are based on trust, respect, and collegiality. Teachers and staff members are more willing to take risks and fear failure less when they have a positive relationship with school leaders.

Teachers and staff members both need to trust that school leaders will be there to catch them should they fail. As school leaders encourage taking risks, they also need to assure teachers and staff members that they will be with them throughout the process. Another key to executing the transformative strategy is to publicly recognize those teachers and staff members who are thinking outside the box, pushing the limits, and taking risks.

Public recognition of innovative and creative teachers and staff members is an effective technique to ensure execution of the change process. Taking the time in a professional learning community or during a faculty meeting to recognize teachers or a staff member will go a long way to growing commitment to change. Furthermore, public recognition of those teachers and staff members who are willing to go beyond the call of duty will lead to others going beyond the call of duty. Public recognition by school leaders is the rubber stamp of approval that teachers and staff members need.

Strategy: Expand Control

> "The only way to make sense out of change is to plunge into it, move with it, and join the dance."
>
> —Alan Watts

There are various forms of school transformation. Some schools choose to perform limited school transformation where only a few school components are changed. Other schools want to focus on whole-school change. Based on our experience, limiting transformation to only individual components within the school will result in short-term gains, but not long-term change. Schools are complex organizations that are made up of many different interconnected moving parts. It is simply not feasible, in our opinion, to focus solely on one component without changing others.

The ultimate purpose of school transformation is to improve outcomes for students by improving a variety of things that are found in schools, such as the teaching and learning process, leadership, culture, operations, policies, and protocols, just to mention a few. Each component mentioned is intertwined and difficult to separate. Think about the many different components that are connected to the teaching and learning process.

In most cases, to change the teaching and learning process, the school's instructional leadership, culture, and systems must also change. It is hard to isolate change to one single component, or even a handful of components. Effective execution of the school's transformation strategy requires that change be comprehensive. High-performing school leaders look at transformation as a means to impact the whole school.

Transformation is used to comprehensively target components that will create lasting school change, even the school leadership. Effective school leaders understand and realize change within the school must keep pace with the speed of change in society. Students today may be globally competitive based on instructional programing, but will the school prepare students to be competitive tomorrow or in the next three, five, or ten years?

Schools must change as students' goals and needs change. Execution of the transformative strategy requires school leaders who are adaptable. Transformative school leaders can only lead change if they themselves embrace change. There is an inherent need for adaptability of school leadership and modeling of change as the transformative strategy is executed.

Strategy: Allocate Time for Change to Occur

"'Too busy' is a myth. People make time for the things that are really important to them."

—Mandy Hale

Throughout the transformative process, many will try to rush the strategy. As we continue to stress, schools are complex organizations, and the transformation process is just as complex. To ensure that change "takes root," time must be allocated to its execution. Furthermore, the transformation process cannot be rushed, even though change is urgently needed. School leaders will need to communicate the importance of giving change time to occur.

Collaboration is key to executing the transformation strategy. The key to collaboration is time. School leaders, teachers, and staff members will need time. In high-performing schools, time is allocated during the school day to allow for vertical and horizontal collaboration. Allocating time for collaboration allows for more people to be at the decision-making table and also helps to build a team within the school that can contribute to effectively executing the transformation strategy.

Creating opportunities for all stakeholders to work together will ensure timely execution of the transformative strategy in the school. Though there will be pressures to speed up the transformation process, we would encourage school leaders to push the brakes. The most effective transformation occurs naturally. Though school leaders ignite the process, change must organically blossom within the school. Organic change, the most effective, is a process that requires time to become infused with the school's DNA.

School leaders will need to be able to understand the importance of timing, as well as recognize when to speed up or slow down execution of the transformation process. School leaders must decisively make decisions that will lead to the best outcomes for the transformation to occur and the decision about the speed of the change. We cannot stress enough that change takes time and each school is different. Therefore, the rate of change will also vary. School leaders must recognize where their school is in regard to the speed needed for change.

Strategy: Reshape the Constructs

"A structure becomes architectural, and not sculptural, when its elements no longer have their justification in nature."

—Guillaume Apollinaire

Most schools are plagued by rigid structures that prevent schools from adapting to current needs. One of the obstacles that keeps school transformation from occurring is the current structures found in schools. The structures that keep change from occurring also prevent collaboration from occurring, impede or discourage shared decision-making, and are nonstudent focused. Schools, like other organizations before transformation, are comfortable with the status quo, favoring comfort over challenges.

For the transformation to be effectively executed, school leaders must come to embrace the understanding that school structures must be reshaped if the change is to occur in schools.

Schools are only going to succeed if structures (constructs) are transformed. At this point, it is important to be clear in regard to what structures impede success. Structures can be physical structures, those visible or invisible day-to-day components of the school operations.

Think about your school. What structures exist in your school that will need to be changed so that the transformation strategy can be executed? Most of the structures that are in schools are from a time defined by a belief that students learn best when in rows with the teacher at the center of the classroom. Now, in today's schools, students expect to be able to work in teams, taught in open and flexible spaces; and to be clear, students are the center of the classroom.

Students are the purpose of learning today; though teachers are important in this overall "school process," they have become facilitators with a sole purpose to help students reach their personalized goals. The necessity to create change and to bend constructs does not pertain to changing the brick, steel, and mortar that is found in schools. School constructs or structures describe bell schedules, policies, instructional programing, lunch programs, transportation, and facility management, all of which are vital to running the school effectively each day.

Consequently, they are also critical to effectively executing the transformation strategy. They are massive and, in most cases, are ingrained into the school's DNA—so changing these components will most certainly be challenging. But in order for change to occur, those structures mentioned will most certainly need to be transformed, whether that transformation is minimally invasive or extensively invasive.

School leaders must recognize that an individual or team has implemented many of the structures that exist in schools for a reason. We mention this because understanding and appreciating this fact will better position the school leader to be able to communicate why changing those structures is needed. Someone or a team created the structure for a reason, so a personal connection to the structure may exist; therefore, individuals or teams may or may not be open to change.

School leaders will need to do their homework to make sure that they understand the reason and purpose for the structure before presenting options for change. Failure to understand the school's constructs is the result of poor planning or a lack of interest in "true" school transformation; it is only a "superficial" type of change at the surface level. Transforming the school's structures is vision critical and is about changing not only the school's components at the surface, but also those components that are ingrained into the DNA of the school.

Each structure (surface or subsurface) needs to be evaluated and assessed to determine alignment to the school's vision and strategy for transformation. Executing the transformative strategy and changing the school's structures will require a high-level of collaboration among school leaders, teachers, and staff members. As school teams will learn, many of the structures are boulders, which will require jackhammers to change or remove.

But, by working together, structures can be transformed. Some structures will be like boulders; however, those too can be transformed, even if it takes a proverbial stick of dynamite. School leaders in combination with a clear vision for change and a collaborative staff can be that stick of dynamite that can create long-term, sustainable transformation! Be persistent as you approach obstacles and turn them into opportunities that will grow the school and your leadership abilities.

Strategy: Own the Vision

"Good business leaders create a vision, articulate the vision, passionately own the vision, and relentlessly drive it to completion."

—Jack Welch

The school's vision, based on our experience, is the most important component of the school's transformation. Likewise, we feel the vision for the transformation strategy plays a crucial role in carrying out the change process. There must be 100 percent commitment to the school's vision and vision for change. School leaders must be the cheerleaders for the vision, as well as the chief enforcers of the vision principles within the school. But, the key is to have a compelling, urgent, purposeful, and relevant school vision and vision for change.

For the school's vision to be effective, the principles must be threaded into the school's change process. The school's vision must define the school and the school's effectiveness or quality. To help make the point, we can look at the story of Alan Mulally's transformation of the Ford Motor Company. The former CEO did a phenomenal job of turning Ford Motor Company around during the recession and was credited as being the chief architect of Ford not accepting a government bailout, while General Motors and Chrysler, on the other hand, did.

Mulally's story is relevant, as he owned the turnaround vision and completely believed in Ford, though he had never worked for Ford or in the automotive industry; in fact, his career was with Boeing, the jet manufacturer. Mulally, in speeches, tells about his first day arriving at Ford Motor Company Headquarters in Dearborn, Michigan. As he pulled into the parking garage, he noticed that no one at the headquarters was driving a Ford.

Mulally says that there were zero Ford vehicles in the parking lot. He speaks about how the first thing in his turnaround plan was to get people to believe in Ford and their products. Without believing in the company, the organization, the school, change will be a wasted, costly, and ineffective process. Mullay's story is provided as an example, as a means to emphasize the need for school leaders, as well as teachers and staff members, to own the school's vision and believe in the school.

School leaders, teachers, and staff members must believe in the school and the quality of instruction and effectiveness of learning. They, too, must also have a laser focus on student success, creating the best learning opportunities and environments possible for students. To effectively execute the transformation strategy, the number of school leaders, teachers, and staff members who believe in the school must far outnumber those who do not believe in the school or see no need for a change.

Yes, believe it or not, there are school leaders, teachers, and staff members who do not fully support the school. They may be visible, or they may lurk in the shadows. Either way, school transformation requires a clear vision and stakeholders who drive a Ford—in other words, who support the school and believe in the school. Effective execution of the transformation strategy will require school leaders to work in close collaboration with other supportive teachers and staff members to help bring those on the other side (nonsupporters) across the divide or assist in transitioning them out of the school.

TRANSFORMATIVE IDEAS FROM THE FIELD

School leaders have a critical task of making sure that the transformation strategy is executed. Yes, they are ultimately responsible for ensuring that change occurs, but before change can happen, they are also responsible for creating a strategy. The key to change is having a clear vision, a strategy, and involving others in carrying out the plan. As mentioned repeatedly throughout *Can Every School Succeed? Bending Constructs to Transform an American Icon*, schools are complex organizations.

There is no reason why school leaders should attempt to lead change in isolation, in fact, change cannot occur in isolation. Though school leaders may initiate the change process at the beginning, they must quickly involve others in the change process and empower them to develop the vision, strategy, and lead the execution of the process. Remember the goal is to execute the transformative strategy almost to perfection, and that will require a team approach.

Too many school leaders attempt to transform schools without a clear strategy. If school leaders have no plan or strategy, then there is no change destination. Without question, without a plan, school transformation will remain elusive or superficial. School transformation is strategic and does not happen by coincidence. There must be a plan, a blueprint that can be monitored and evaluated for success. Executing a strategy for change provides benchmarks that are visible, impactful, and transformative. All of which can be assessed for success, measured against outcomes for student success.

PRINCIPAL'S NOTES

"However beautiful the strategy, you should occasionally look at the results." —Sir Winston Churchill

4:30 p.m.
February 10
Leadership Team Meeting—Library
Spring Water Elementary School

We were heading into the second half of the school year. The staff was in the middle of implementing new instructional strategies, utilizing cutting edge educational technology, looking at data in innovative ways, and, most importantly, having a good time doing it. With teachers and administrators from all over the district coming to view our new practices, it was vital that we could back up our work with results. It would do our students absolutely no good to put together a showy new instructional program that looked great on the surface, but yielded zero results.

It was time to conduct a data comparison to previous years and cohorts of students. Some schools looked at achievement data by only comparing this year's third-grade cohort to last year's third-grade cohort. We knew that this method was a mistake. You must also compare apples to apples, or plainly speaking, look at the same students over time. My leadership team was in charge of creating data sheets for their grade levels in the following areas: benchmark academic progress, attendance, and discipline. Each teacher leader had five minutes to share out their data.

The results were jaw-dropping.

Grade levels that were implementing the vision had results that were unheard of in past years. Individual students in classrooms that had historically struggled in school were now on grade level for the first time in their lives. Disciplinary incidents were way down due to students not wanting to miss out on classroom activities. Attendance was up for the same reason.

Sadly, other grade levels did not have the same results. In fact, two grade levels had flatlined. Excuses were made, but they fell on deaf ears. There was a lot of finger pointing at students and parents. We had been down this tired road before. It was time for some crucial conversations.

I set up meetings with these grade levels individually. I had crafted an agenda ahead of time and asked each teacher to bring their data.

I also brought in some data that I had been collecting. Over the last several months, I had been compiling walk-through data. I was keeping track of different instructional elements, such as seating arrangements, student engagement, student and teacher actions, use of technology, differentiation, and student output. First, I showed the school-wide walk-through data.

Then, I unpacked it by grade level. The differences were clear. The data from grade levels that showed me the most growth indicated high levels of student engagement; active teaching and learning; differentiation for English Language Learners, students with disabilities, and intervention students; as well as, high uses of technology; flexible seating arrangements; and student work output that included project-based learning, collaborations, and high level of problem solving. The data from the grade levels that underperformed indicated low levels of these elements.

Although the vision was set and tools for improvement were made available, the execution of the vision was not made with fidelity. We needed to restart, regroup, and move forward. Longtime UCLA basketball coach John Wooden once said, "Never mistake activity for achievement." I didn't want my teachers to just go through the motions; I wanted them to engage.

I worked with these teachers to create some short-term goals. I was in their classrooms on a daily basis. I spent my time over the next few weeks modeling, coaching, and demonstrating what was working in other classrooms. There were tears, frustration, and questions about the legitimacy of our vision. I pressed on like this for several weeks.

Then, they saw the results.

Our formative data indicated that the students in these classes were catching on and moving closer to content proficiency. I shared this data with the entire staff, celebrating the hard work of these teachers. Gone were the tears of frustration and in came tears of joy and satisfaction. They had executed the vision with rigor and fidelity. Our staff was now one cohesive unit with a shared vision at the heart of our work.

The challenge that was now presented to us was to sustain this positive forward momentum.

TAKEAWAY IDEAS

- Change must begin with a clear vision and executable strategy.
- Executing a change strategy provides a means to monitor and evaluate success.
- Recognize change agents in the school who are assisting with executing the strategy for transformation.
- School leaders, teachers, and staff members must believe in the school, before they can believe in the transformation process.
- Strategic transformation encompasses all school structures to create lasting change.
- Own and believe in the vision.
- Be, and empower others to be, the dynamite that removes boulders that impede school transformation.

Chapter Eight

Sustainability

Going Beyond Tomorrow

Sustainability

School transformation is not a process that has a start and finish line; instead, it is a continuous, cyclical process. The most important takeaway is that for public schools to remain relevant in today's increasingly competitive landscape, change must be sustainable. Change that is needed in today's schools to make public schools relevant must be continuous. Additionally, as transformation becomes embedded into the school's culture and day-to-day operations, the sustainability of the change processes becomes sustainable.

The importance of creating change that is lasting and adaptable cannot be emphasized enough. School leaders, working closely with teachers and staff members, must work to build change within the school that is strategic, scalable, and sustainable. We often find that change occurs and then stakeholders lose focus. But, in fact, school transformation requires constant monitoring, evaluating, and modifying as needs change in schools.

Schools are changing rapidly due to various reasons, including student demographics, teacher demographics, accountability requirements, school budgets, and much more. As schools will remain in a constant state of change over the foreseeable future, transforming the structures, systems, protocols, and processes must be aligned to the school's strategic plan. Transformation, within a school, that is not in line with the school's long-term strategy, vision, or goals will not be sustainable.

In simple terms, sustaining the school's transformation requires that change is aligned with current or future needs and the school's long-term strategy. Schools elect to go through a transformative journey as a means to meet the needs of students, including their academic and social needs, aspirations, and long-term goals. Once change occurs, it must be sustained.

TRANSFORMATION CORE IDEA

School transformation must be *sustainable*. Creating a culture that embraces the continuous improvement process is critical to sustainability and reinforces the commitment to the change process into the future.

> For change to truly be transformative it must be part of the school's DNA. In other words, transformation must be sustainable well into the future. Sustainability is largely determined by the school's willingness and ability to implement systems that ensure that the components of change are interconnected with the school's strategic plan. The commitment of school leaders, teachers, and staff members to engage in ongoing professional learning strengthens the school's ability for school transformation, resulting in long-term growth in student achievement. Just as professional learning is important, the school leaders' willingness to engage in continuous improvement—that is, identifying strengths and gaps—strengthens the transformation plan for sustainability.

TRANSFORMATIVE KEY UNDERSTANDINGS

- *The Journey Continues*—School transformation is measured by sustained student achievement. School leaders must work toward ensuring that teachers and staff members do not focus on a destination, but help them to recognize that transformation is a journey.
- *Transparency*—One of the greatest strategies school leaders can use is to keep stakeholders informed about the school's progress, trials, setbacks, and how they can be involved. Transparency is key to stakeholders trusting the school's leadership and sustaining change.
- *Community Support*—Next to transparency is the continued support from the community. School leaders must work diligently to maintain community support for school transformation. Without community support, transformation cannot be sustained.

- *Fear and Recognize Complacency*—As schools begin to experience success through the change process, school leaders must keep everyone moving forward, striving to reach new higher levels of excellence for students. Complacency works against sustained school transformation.
- *The Embrace of Teachers and Staff*—School leaders must ensure that teachers and staff support the transformation process. They must recruit and retain teachers and staff members who support and embrace the transformation process.
- *Ownership*—School leadership must continue to make the transformation part of the school's vision and aligned to the needs of the school. Stakeholders must see transformation as needed and aligned to what they want in a school, remaining focused on ensuring student success and preparedness for the next level.

TRANSFORMATIVE ROLES

School Leaders:

- Recognize the need for a clear, simple, and sustainable plan for transformation;
- Commit resources and supports for continuous improvement;
- Establish need for ongoing professional learning and provide opportunities that will help sustain school transformation;
- Develop long-term goals that can help measure growth and sustainability.

Teachers and Staff Members:

- View transformation as a journey and not a destination;
- Establish goals that focus on long-term student success and preparedness;
- Self-assess preparedness and growth for continued transformation;
- Ensure that transformation always is student-centered.

RESEARCH AND TRANSFORMATION

As we begin the final step in the process of school transformation, research is unequivocal that there is no end to transforming schools. All the more reason why sustainability is the last step that we present. To make it easier, we feel that sustainability should be viewed through the lens of continuous improvement, which is an integral component of organizational change. Based on our experiences, sustainability is often overlooked in school transformation. Most school leaders rarely think about the long-term impact of change. They think of how to keep change moving even less.

The sustainability of school transformation may be overwhelming to many school leaders, teachers, and staff members. At some point, a member or members of the team will say something like this, "You want us to change, and you now are asking that we keep change going." A question like this will certainly be asked because change is hard even in the simplest terms. To reduce the pushback among stakeholders, we encourage school leaders to invite feedback and input.

According to Bass and Rubin (2012), buy-in and ownership will help keep the change process on a sustainable path. Bass and Rubin's research is consistent with why we have emphasized buy-in, shared decision-making, and engagement of diverse perspectives throughout the previous chapters. Without buy-in, transformation will not succeed; therefore, sustainability becomes a moot point.

Through research, we also discover another key strategy to ensuring the transformation persists in the future. According to Greenhalgh, MacFarlane, Barton-Sweeney, and Woodard (2012), "weaving" change into the organization's culture leads to continuous improvement. In schools that have successfully transformed, change still occurs. The transformation of the school into an organization focused on student success continues three, five, and ten years from the start of the process.

Why? The reason is that school leaders at these schools understood that stakeholders must not only embrace change, but also be part of how the school conducts day-to-day business. Change is not only embraced, but encouraged daily as a sustainable means to exist. One component that we feel will lead to the greatest results throughout the transformation process and also the inevitable sustainability of school change is the commitment of school leaders.

Just as school leaders are the gatekeepers to many things in school, including change, they too determine the impact of long-term strategic change. According to Brannmark and Benn (2012), leadership's ownership of change is a key determinant of success. We argue that without the school leaders' support, commitment, and persistence, the transformation will not succeed, nor will it continue.

Many schools go through the transformation process, only to see their principal leave or ultimately fail. Most school principals, we find, rarely stay to see the transformation of the school through. When this happens, a new school principal is hired and either stops the transformation process by choice, unknowingly, or begins the school on a different journey. Here again, we make the argument that change must be ingrained into the school's culture, which will help keep change moving, with or without a school principal.

TRANSFORMATIVE POINTS TO CONSIDER

- Transforming a school is one thing; keeping the school moving in a positive direction is an entirely different topic. School transformation and sustainability is rarely discussed, as school administrators are focused on present change, which is why change is urgently needed now. But in fact, transformation is both a short and long-term process. Change is not a destination, but a continual cycle of improvement.
- School leaders throughout the transformation process must think how change will continue. Schools do not only begin the transformation process to address the present problems in schools, but also the problems in the future. School administrators are encouraged to focus on continuous improvement as a means to help keep the transformation process going.
- Once school leaders decide to begin the transformation process in their schools, they must follow through with the change. Programs, systems, and plans that are rarely completed plague schools for the long-term. Transformation is something that must continue moving forward. Transformation is not something that starts and stops, based on the mood of school leaders, teachers, and staff members. Once transformation begins, push forward and keep working at it no matter the challenge, setback, or obstacle.
- Transformation is best described as a cycle with no end. Educators like starting and ending points, but in regards to transformation, there is a start, but rarely does transformation have a finish line. There are always opportunities for change. School leaders must think about how change will look tomorrow and the next day. The evaluation of how effective the transformation process is will be measured by the school's ability to continue the change process into the future and how ingrained the change is in the school's culture.

PRACTICAL INTRODUCTION

School transformation is useless if it is not sustainable for the long-term. Sustainability must be an integral part of the transformation discussion from the beginning. As schools prepare for school transformation they must also make preparation for how the change will continue and evolve as needed. School transformation is not just one of those day-to-day decisions made by school leaders. Instead, school transformation is a long-term strategic process that becomes part of the school's DNA and vision for the long-term.

School transformation often fails in schools when school leaders, teachers, and staff members fail to plan for the long-term. The ability to continue, even if a school leader leaves, is essential to the effectiveness of school transformation. Sustainability will be determined by how well the school leader engages and empowers others to be part of the process and they, collaboratively, engrain into the school's culture, structures, day-to-day process, the school's DNA.

The more the school sticks with the transformation, the more comfortable school leaders, teachers, and staff members will be as change begins. There must be a clear understanding that once change starts, change can't stop. School transformation is not an easy process. Long-term change is a strategic process that is supported and embraced by all stakeholders. If change occurs, which must be celebrated, stakeholders will want to keep the changes and look for opportunities to expand the successes, which requires sustainability.

The goal of transformation is to make changes that will result in long-term student success and preparedness at the next level. Sustainability is key to helping students achieve long-term; it is achieved by school leaders, teachers, and school staff having the capacity to bring about and maintain change. School leaders without a strategy to sustain the transformation for the long-haul should not begin the change process.

KEY QUESTIONS

The Key Questions are meant to help school leaders begin thinking about the transformation principles in relation to their schools.

- What is your school's plan for sustaining the transformation?
- How will the school measure the sustainability of the transformation strategy?
- What are the school's next steps in the transformation process?
- How will the school's transformation strategy be adapted over the short and long-term? What is the process?
- As a school leader, how will you keep stakeholders engaged in the transformation process and sustaining the school's success?

SUSTAINABILITY TRANSFORMED

Strategy: Openly Communicate and Keep Stakeholders Informed

"The art of communication is the language of leadership."

—James Humes

The last phase of school transformation is just as important as the first step, which is establishing a school vision. As school leaders begin to develop a plan for sustainability, there must be an open dialogue with stakeholders and a school culture of transparency. School leaders, teacher leaders, and other leaders must be prepared to keep open lines of communication throughout the transformation process.

The reason? Open dialogue and transparency help stakeholders to remain committed to the transformation process and ensure that the change created continues into the future. Transparency helps to strengthen the change occurring in the school. Instead of change occurring in the shadows, change should be a team effort that is open for the entire school community to see. Transformation is too important to be decided on behind closed doors. The more decisions are made in the open and through collaboration, the stronger the sustainability of the changes that occur.

School leaders, in cooperation with teachers and staff members, can utilize a variety of strategies to share data and information with stakeholders even as the transformation process comes to an end. Regular communication, each week, biweekly, or at least monthly will help keep stakeholders focused on the vision and goals for change. Regularly sharing processes, metrics, areas of concerns, and next steps will help stakeholders remain committed to the process. Furthermore, they will continue to trust the process. Often, the transformation process is derailed during times of setbacks because stakeholders lose confidence in the process.

Regular communication and dialogue with stakeholders will keep stakeholders believing in the process. School leaders need to communicate clearly that setbacks, challenges, and barriers are all part of the transformation process. Change is never perfect, and with school leaders sharing this information throughout the process, more stakeholders will remain committed to the process. If stakeholders receive missing information or misinformation, the transformation process is questioned, which can impact the overall results.

As school leaders, the following strategies can be utilized to create a clear and straightforward communication pipeline to sustain change.

- Even as change comes to an end, remind stakeholders of why the change was and is still needed.
  - Stakeholders often forget change is an ongoing process. Moreover, as the transformation process continues, many fail to remember why the change was necessary. School leaders must consistently communicate the journey, where the school started, where the school is currently, and where the school is going. More importantly, why change is still needed.
- Regularly communicate that change is an ongoing process.
  - School transformation is a continuous process, often a cycle. Think about a five-year strategic plan. As schools reach the end of the five-year strategic plan, they begin to think about the next five years. With each passing day, the needs of students change and become more diversified. Change must be sustained as a means to meet the changes that are occurring in the school.
- Seek regular feedback and input from stakeholders.
  - Change continues as a result of stakeholders being engaged in the process. For stakeholders to remain committed to and involved in the transformation of the school, school leaders need to regularly provide opportunities for stakeholders to provide input, feedback, and make decisions. School leaders need to hear from stakeholders throughout the process and as change goes forward. Stakeholders need to feel comfortable sharing their experiences, their ups and downs, as well as their needs throughout the change process. All of this helps to keep stakeholders committed to the continual change process.
- Keep change exciting and vision critical.
  - School transformation is exciting as change occurs and a sense of newness spreads throughout the school. School leaders will almost certainly face the time when the excitement for change wears off. Additionally, stakeholders will be complacent, comfortable where they are and less willing to change as the transformation process continues. School leaders will need to utilize strategic spontaneity: shaking up change while remaining committed to the overall vision for change. Just because a change process worked once is not a guarantee the process will work later on.
- Be transparent with information, even the setbacks, barriers, and challenges; transparency builds trust in the process.
  - Though transparency is critical throughout the process, freely sharing information is essential to sustaining change moving forward. As transformation progresses, sharing information keeps stakeholders engaged and committed to the change that is occurring and also to the change that is still needed. School leaders will need to utilize strategies that make

information accessible to stakeholders quickly and freely, without barriers and in real-time. Transparency throughout the change process helps to silence the noises from those who doubt change is occurring and also contributes to validating the work of those who support change.

- Form teams made up of stakeholders and empower them with data and the responsibility of sharing it with others.
  - Shared decision-making is often overlooked, underestimated, and undervalued. Too many schools begin the transformation process without understanding the importance of stakeholder empowerment and shared leadership. Furthermore, as the transformation process continues, team decision-making sometimes falls to the side and becomes less necessary. We encourage shared decision-making and the use of school leadership teams as a means to keep change moving and sustaining the changes that have occurred. The team, not just school leaders, can help keep change moving forward.

Stakeholders must understand that the transformation of the school is an ongoing process. As the school transforms, change must continue, as the needs of students, teachers, staff members, and other stakeholders will continue to change. For change to continue, school leaders, just as they did in the early stages of the transformation process, will need to be leading the charge and empowering others to be leaders.

Open dialogue about the need for continued change is critical to school transformation. No organization has ever failed when they were transparent with stakeholders about the organization's focus, vision, and goals. However, many organizations have failed as a result of decisions being made in the shadows and stakeholders kept from being part of the process. If decisions are customarily made in the shadows in your school, quickly bring the decision-making process out in the open for everyone to see and be part of.

Strategy: Systematically Monitor Performance

"Effective leaders also understand that alignment is not something to check off a to-do list. Alignment is dynamic, ongoing process that requires continual monitoring and realigning as conditions and needs change."

—Talent Gear

Often, school transformation is discussed without mentioning the need to systematically monitor performance or the change that has occurred. Based on our experiences, we feel that ongoing monitoring and evaluating change is a critical component that leads to the sustainability of change in schools.

School leaders, along with others, need to monitor and assess the transformation progress.

By doing so, transformation remains at the forefront of school decisions and in the minds of stakeholders. Just like all other components and processes in schools, transformation must also be monitored and evaluated for continued alignment to the school's vision and goals. More importantly, it must be monitored to ensure that the outcomes are resulting in positive effects for students. Transformation is about creating the best outcomes for students, period!

Below are key considerations as schools begin to monitor the transformation process and school performance systematically. The importance of tracking the transformation's progress cannot be understated. It is the responsibility of school leaders to work with teachers and staff members to develop monitoring processes that will help the school to achieve the overall goal: increased student success, through organizational transformation. As you begin, consider the following:

- Regularly monitor the school's performance that is shared with stakeholders.
- Strategically establish an evaluation process for change and performance that is aligned with the school's overall goals.
- Regularly communicate the school's vision and goals for the transformation process. Discuss monitoring data as a team where school leaders, teachers, and staff members collaboratively decide next steps, areas of strength, and areas for improvement.
- Be focused on addressing strengths and areas for improvement. Too often, the areas of improvement are the focus of school transformation. However, for sustainability purposes, both the good and bad need to be evaluated and monitored frequently.
- Utilize longitudinal data. Analyzing present data with longitudinal data helps to sustain the focus of the transformation process. Furthermore, past, present, and future data must be compared to the transformation goals that have been established by the team. Know where the school is and where the school is going at all times to ensure the sustainability of the transformation process.
- Create and utilize a simple tool for monitoring that can be used by school leaders, teachers, and staff members. The goal is to efficiently collect and analyze data, which must be compared to the overall goals of the transformation process.
- Seek input and feedback from all school stakeholders on how best to evaluate and analyze the school's performance and strategic goals. The more vested the stakeholders are in the process, the more sustainable the transformation can be in the school.

The intensity of data sharing will need to be aligned to the needs of the school. Some schools will need weekly updates about the change process, while others may only need quarterly updates. School leaders will need to work closely with stakeholders within the school to determine how often data is shared. Systematically monitoring and evaluating the transformation process helps to keep change relevant to the needs of the students, stakeholders, and the school.

School leaders can use the data to make corrections in the transformation strategy, in real-time. For change to remain relevant in schools, change needs to occur based on current requirements found within the school, as well as future needs. Don't be afraid to assess the school to identify what is working and what needs to be improved. Better yet, involve others in helping you to assess the school and identify next steps to creating sustainable change.

Strategy: Keep It Simple

"Make it simple, but significant."

—Don Draper

Change is hard in any organization, largely as a result of those who work in the organizations. Schools are no different; change is and will be difficult. To lessen the complexities and to keep change sustainable, the change process needs to be simple. Simple does not mean that change can't be transformative, just that change needs to be strategic, simple, and understood by all. Furthermore, change must be made relevant to stakeholders. Stakeholders are not going to buy-in or commit to something that they do not see as necessary or that they don't understand.

Sustainable transformation requires that stakeholders change mindsets, starting with school leaders. School leaders must develop the mindset that for change to occur, a collaborative leadership approach is required. As we have tried to convey throughout previous chapters, the school transformation process is complex and isolated leadership will not be conducive to creating the change needed in schools.

School leaders must realize that shared, collaborative leadership does not lessen their effectiveness, but when expertly executed, collaborative leadership structures can improve the effectiveness of school leadership and the performance of the school. But keep in mind, the most effective forms of leadership are always simple, never fancy, and never complicated. The most effective school leaders are natural leaders who lead without the need for fancy offices, complex organizational structures, and they never lead in isolation.

The mindset of teachers and staff members will also need to be changed. Teachers and staff members must have the mindset that change can occur through collaboration. A change in mindset among teachers and staff members can be achieved through open dialogue and empowerment. Updates, as a result of change, good or bad, must be shared with stakeholders as often as possible.

Transparency helps to build trust while also showing that change can occur in the school. By providing regular updates about the change that is happening, school leaders will help many of the stakeholders who doubt the transformation process begin to buy-in to the approach. Buy-in from stakeholders contributes to continuing the change process going forward. No organization fails when decisions and information are transparent.

A growth mindset is essential to keeping the transformation process simple. Based on our experience, as school leaders, having a growth mindset helps to reduce many of the complexities involved in change, such as reluctance to change, negativity toward change, and lack of confidence in the ability to change. All three only add unnecessary layers to the transformation that can complicate the change that is needed in schools.

Think about how simple the transformation process could be if all stakeholders supported change, had a positive view toward change, and had the confidence to be change agents. Buy-in can be achieved in multiple ways such as transparency of information, but also by keeping the change process simple. Schools are already complex, so look for ways to reduce the complexities, not add to them.

Though urgency to change exists in schools, school leaders need to understand that quality is far more important than speed. School leaders must recognize that changing mindsets does not occur on a fixed timetable. There will need to be dialogue, education, and patience. By engaging teachers and staff members in the discussion about the transformation process, school leaders will save a lot of time, energy, and cost in the long-term. Never underestimate the power of simplicity and empowerment on transforming a school and increasing student achievement.

Effective long-term transformation extends well into the future of the school and can be achieved by putting change in terms that are relevant and understood by stakeholders. Too often, school leaders try to do large-scale change by throwing too many moving parts at stakeholders. We see it all the time when school leaders attend professional development and then go back to school and try to implement the program or strategy.

Transformation must be strategic and requires that capacity is built along the way that is aligned with the changes that are needed. School leaders need to recognize that teachers and staff members, as well as other stakeholders can only take so much change at one time. Schools that utilize a phase-in approach to change are successful at connecting the dots between each transformation component and also keep change simple. Often, transformation remains complex as too much change is attempted at one time, while "phasing" can help keep change simple.

TRANSFORMATIVE IDEAS FROM THE FIELD

Change is an ongoing, continuous process that can lead to long-term student success. As schools begin the transformation process, sustainability, that is the process of keeping change relevant and moving forward, must be at the forefront of the decision making process and be considered as changes begin to occur. How will changes be sustained going forward? As the transformation process begins, school leaders, teachers, and staff members must focus on creating change that is sustainable. Nonstrategic changes are short-term and rarely sustainable. Change must be integral to the school's long-term strategy, but also adaptable to the needs within the school, specifically the needs of students.

Sustainability requires that transformation is strategic and aligned to the school's overall vision and goals. Change must occur based on the need and the desire to reach higher levels of success and improve the school's performance for students. Transformation is all about the school's continuous improvement process geared toward student success. The more school leaders, teachers, and staff members can keep change tied directly to making improvements that will lead to increases in student success, the more sustainable the change will be.

If stakeholders see the results of the change that have occurred through the lens of student success, their long-term support will be strengthened and sustained. School transformation is hard, as we have continued to state throughout the book. Equally difficult is the process of sustaining the changes that have occurred in the school. Too often, change occurs, and stakeholders within the school quickly forget, and many of the old processes or "way things have already been done" mindsets return.

From the beginning, the transformation process must be put in cyclical terms, a continuous improvement process, with an understanding that change will always be needed in schools. Always start change, never stop changing. Maintain a laser focus on student success and as school leaders, teachers, and staff members, you will be effective in your pursuit to create a school that is student-centered.

PRINCIPAL'S NOTES

*"My buildings will be my legacy. . . they will speak
for me long after I'm gone."* —Julia Morgan

2:45 p.m.
June 9
Library
Spring Water Elementary School

The school year was coming to an end. It had been a long, difficult, and yet rewarding year. We had come a long way in just nine months. There were plenty of tears, laughter, discovery, fear, and joy that followed us on our collective journey. For the first time in recent memory, the staff was a cohesive unit that shared a collective vision of excellence for the school.

Risks were taken, lessons were learned, adjustments made, and goals obtained. I was exhausted. We were all exhausted. There's a saying in sports: we left it all out on the field. With the first year at Spring Water Elementary School in the books, I began to contemplate my future. I knew that there so much more to accomplish. I also understood that education is constantly changing and that we needed to be ready for what was coming around the bend.

I also knew that to be successful in the future, I needed to ensure the following notions:

1. I needed to continue to foster capacity in my teacher leaders. That would be one of the most important means to sustain our momentum and growth.
2. Continue to be transparent with data. Data should always be used to inform our practice. We should never shy away from the good, the bad, or the ugly. It all makes us better educators. There are learning opportunities in all of them.
3. Set long-term goals with shorter, obtainable goals in the middle. It was important to be able to celebrate victories along the way, rather than set lofty goals that seemed out of reach.

It also became apparent that we had to focus on hiring the right teaches for the right positions. We needed educators who embraced innovation and change, not the status quo. We were building a legacy.

None of us were going to work at Spring Water forever. All of us, at some point, would either retire, move, or look for other opportunities. We needed the vision of the school to be bigger than the individuals working at it at that given time.

Each new hire would need to be carefully selected so that they would comfortably thrive within the vision, while not being afraid to change it in the future. Maintaining the status quo was not something that we were interested in doing. We wanted to continue to be challenged and inspire one another. The same is true of families. They must be equal partners in carrying this torch forward. This notion was instilled in everything we did. It was vital that we continued to reach out to local businesses, community members, and elected officials.

Through this process I have realized that school leadership has three major elements. I call them the Three Ps: people, process, and product. After a year's worth of work, we now had the right people, engaged in the right work, in order to fulfill the right vision we had crafted together. Without this triad of excellence, a school would never be able to fulfill its vision or reach its potential.

People. Process. Product.

That is the recipe for sustainability.

TAKEAWAYS IDEAS

- School transformation is a continuous process.
- Transparency is key to sustaining change in schools.
- Create a process to monitor and evaluate the transformation process to ensure continued alignment to the school's vision and long-term goals.
- Keep change simple and strategic, which will help to reduce the complexities that often come with change.
- Encourage stakeholder involvement and input throughout the transformation process as a way to sustain the change processes implemented.

Conclusion

"If you want to succeed, stop reading inspirational quotes and get to work."

—Guy Kawasaki

To all those school leaders who doubt their ability to create change, remember that all great journeys begin by taking the first step. As we have conveyed throughout *Can Every School Succeed? Bending Constructs to Transform an American Icon*, schools must transform and reduce the complexities that are currently preventing many of them from changing. The complexities such as rigid school policies, structures that discourage collaboration, and high-stakes accountability models are slowly suffocating public education today.

As school leaders, we have the chance to transform schools going forward, if we are willing to embrace change as an engine for peak organizational performance. Too many schools begin the transformation process without a clear understanding of the purpose of creating change. No matter the reason behind why a school starts the transformation process, change must be initiated to help students. In other words, school transformation is always about creating the best learning opportunities and environment for students.

Though there may be particular operational issues and instructional challenges that need to be addressed, at the end of the day, schools must begin the transformation process with a laser focus on student success. As in all decisions made in school, students must be at the heart of school transformation—changing constructs, mindsets, and processes that will lead to all students being prepared for college, a career, and for life. Educators must never forget that the success of students must always be weighed in all decisions.

Throughout *Can Every School Succeed?* we have introduced school leaders to transformative principles, that, based on our experience, are critical to creating the change needed in schools. Each principle provides school leaders, teachers, and staff members an opportunity to transform their school from being focused on other things besides student success. In the end, transformation helps schools to return to the basis of teaching and learning: students.

Schools today must change and realize how important student success is. We no longer can afford to target student success through outdated processes and protocols that were developed decades earlier. Today's students demand and expect a certain level of personalization. That is, students want schools that address their individual needs, goals, and aspirations.

Our goal throughout this book is to encourage school leaders to rethink the school process. As school leaders, we have probably what is a moral responsibility to change the school process today to meet the needs of students. In our opinion, the level of change in schools may vary; however, all schools need to change. Many schools are doing a phenomenal job at preparing students for success and ensuring their readiness at the next level.

Without a commitment to or embrace of continuous improvement and transformation, those schools will eventually begin to struggle to meet the growing demands of students or the changing needs of students. As we have tried to stress throughout *Can Every School Succeed?* though the transformation process begins with school leaders, they alone do not share the burden to create lasting change alone.

For transformation to be effective and sustainable, school leaders must engage and empower others to be part of improving the school. School leaders, teachers, and staff members must own and lead the transformation process. There must be a certain level of commitment to changing the school to become more effective at preparing students. Schools must become organizations with unparalleled student satisfaction and success.

School transformation can occur in any school, though some schools will experience failure, setbacks, and challenges. But what we have learned, through our experiences and interactions with other school leaders, teachers, and staff members in other schools, is that those schools that turn failure into learning opportunities are those schools that have successful transformation experiences.

There are too many school leaders, teachers, and staff members who allow setbacks and challenges to derail their school's journey. Change is never easy, and school-wide change will test the resolve of many. However, schools must keep moving forward, no matter the setback or obstacle. Each challenge or setback provides schools opportunities to grow the stamina needed to become more flexible . . . and better for students.

The greater the scale of the transformation that occurs in the school, the greater the impact on students. We encourage school leaders not to focus solely on one school process, system, or department, but the entire school as an organization. All components found in a school are interconnected, making it difficult or impossible to isolate change to one area. As schools begin the transformation process, look to focus on school-wide change.

If the transformation process is taken seriously and viewed as a positive process, there will be many processes and systems that will be changed, while some will be identified as effective and only strengthened throughout the change process. Schools must change and become places of personalized learning. School leaders must lead the movement to challenge the status quo and create centers of learning that focus on the needs, goals, and aspirations of all students.

Organizational change will undoubtedly be challenging for most schools, but schools can succeed. In fact, schools must succeed! Students' readiness and eventual competitiveness on the global stage depends on schools' ability to meet their academic needs today. Meeting the diverse needs of students will only occur if schools fundamentally change the entire school process. Schools can no longer focus on creating systems centered on the masses, but instead, centered on the individual student.

You, the school leader, the teacher, or the staff member are on the verge of beginning a transformative journey. As the school begins the transformation process, you will change the school but also learn about your role in the school and ways to become more effective. We challenge the notion that transformation is isolated to only the organization. In our experience, school transformation touches each stakeholder, leading to professional growth and improved effectiveness in their roles. The key is to be willing to change throughout the transformation process; be open and willing to go where the journey takes you.

Be willing to go where the transformative journey takes the school. Schools have an incredible opportunity to transform and be centers of learning for all students. To reach every student and help them achieve their dreams, schools must begin the transformation process without preconceived limits. Allow the transformation process to be as big or small as needed, based on the needs of students. Every school can succeed, if schools focus on ensuring every student succeeds, which is the purpose of the transformation process.

As presented in *Can Every School Succeed?* school transformation is a universal process, that must be tailored to the needs found in each school. Real and practical school transformation does not follow a cookie-cutter approach, though there are certain principles that are found in all successful changes in schools. Based on our experiences those principles are:

Journey Empowerment Capacity Sustainability

| V | J | B | E | C | C | E | S |

Vision   Buy-in   Change   Execution

- *Vision:* Begin with inspiring school vision, focused on student success that encourages transformation.
- *Journey:* Create a plan that creates school-wide change focused on creating centers of learning focused on the needs of all students.
- *Buy-In:* Encourage and engage others in transforming the school.
- *Empowerment:* Empower others to be change leaders.
- *Change:* Create change that is focused on improving outcomes for students.
- *Capacity:* Grow the ability to change within the school and extending the leadership bench.
- *Execution:* Implement the change strategy that will lead to improved learning environment and opportunities for students.
- *Sustainability:* Ensure lasting change in schools.

There is no better day than today to begin the transformation journey. Start strong so that the school finishes strong and students succeed. Students need schools that have a laser focus on their success. But more importantly, students need school leaders, teachers, and staff members who continually improve. We must never stop growing and seeking opportunities to improve our practice. Society today gives schools the opportunity to educate tomorrow's future.

As educators and school leaders, we have a responsibility to create the best opportunities for students each day. Though we have a responsibility to create change, we also have a chance to do something amazing. Our students count on us to dare fate and to take risks that will help them to reach their dreams and aspire to be even greater. Though the challenge to transform the school may seem daunting and even impossible, take the first step.

No school transformation is perfect or blemish-free, but it can be empowering if embraced. Remember you are not alone and no matter how unsure you are, be confident in your ability to be transformative. Students need you to pave a path to helping them to accomplish their dreams. Can every school succeed? You bet! More importantly, schools must succeed as students' futures are dependent upon on their success.

Begin your school's transformative journey today!

Afterword

Times of challenge invariably come with the opportunity for great gain. Schools now face pressures from every side. With so many facets clamoring for attention it would be easy to despair or give in to the temptation to tread water until the stressors move on. However, the innovations, ideas, and leadership that will transform our schools into the successful institutes of education for the future will come from the "boots on the ground." The principals, teachers, administrators, and support staff who have daily contact with the people our schools are meant to serve: students.

Though schools face unprecedented pressures to succeed, the overwhelming majority are helping students to achieve their academic goals and aspirations. Today's schools are fortunate to have many great leaders, teachers, and support staff that come to work each day with the sole purpose of inspiring greatness in students. This inspiration is what *Can Every School Succeed? Bending Constructs to Transform an American Icon* tries to convey. Brian K. Creasman, Jesse Bacon, and David Franklin have made it clear that schools must be centers of inspiration and innovation for students.

No matter what schools may face, as school leaders, teachers, and support staff, we must remain committed to student success by all means necessary. Students need school leaders, teachers, and support staff to have a laser focus on their success and have a determined mindset and belief in their ability to succeed. School transformation, based on my experience, is creating strategic change that will lead to improved student achievement.

We must not forget that transformation, along with the teaching and learning process and day-to-day school decisions, must be about doing what is best for students. At times, too many lose sight that "school" in all senses of the word is about students and as the authors pointed out several times, schools can't succeed without student success. Simple, yet powerful words to lead and teach by each day.

Schools today have an excellent opportunity to transform; in fact, students are demanding change. Transformation provides an opportunity to create an environment in which our students can thrive. Schools must become student-centered places that encourage young people to embrace education and take what they learn and apply it with their own innovations.

Can every school succeed? Based on my many years of experience as a teacher and school and district leader, they can if schools are about student success. The points of consideration in this book provide a game plan that leaders can use to chart the course for the education of tomorrow. I challenge school leaders, teachers, and support staff to remain positive, student-centered, and determined.

Though your work sometimes goes without notice or recognition, I applaud each of you for what you do for students. Never doubt your impact on student achievement. A single hello in the morning, pat on the back when students experience failure, or words of praise when students win, though small, are powerful in the lives of our students. Positivity has been proven to improve organizational culture, morale, and student achievement.

I challenge you to begin the transformative journey as a vehicle that will lead to a more effective teaching and learning process that is focused on the individual student. Don't ever give up on trying to reach every student and helping them to achieve their dreams as someone did for you and me. You have the opportunity to do something great for students; don't allow this opportunity to get away from you and your school. The time to begin that journey is today.

> Dr. Randy Poe
> Superintendent
> Boone County Schools, Kentucky

Bibliography

SETTING THE STAGE

Creasman, B., and Coquyt, M. (2016). *The Leader Within: Understanding and Empowering Teacher Leaders*. Lanham, MD: Rowman and Littlefield Publishers.

Leithwood, K. & Jantzi, D. (2006). Transformational School Leadership for Large-Scale Reform: Effects on Students, Teachers, and their Classroom Practice. *School Effectiveness and School Improvement*, 17 (2) 201–227.

Matveev, A., and Lvina, E. (2007). Effective transformational leadership across cultures: The role of cross communication competence. Paper presented at WCA Conference, Brisbane.

Yukl, G. (1999). An evaluation of conceptual weaknesses in transformational and charismatic leadership theories. *Leadership Quarterly, 10*, 285–305.

CHAPTER 1: VISION

Huffman, J. B., and Hipp, K. A. (2001). Creating communities of learners: The interaction of shared leaders, shared vision, and supportive conditions. *International Journal of Educational Reform, 10*(3), 272–81.

Kotter, J. P. (1997). Leading by vision and strategy. *Executive Excellence, 14*(10), 15–16.

Schneider, B., Brief, A. P., and Guzzo, R. A. (1996). Creating a climate and culture for sustainable organizational change. *Organizational Dynamics, 24*(4), 7–19.

CHAPTER 2: JOURNEY

Benefiel, M. (2005). The second half of the journey: Spiritual leadership for organizational transformation. *Leadership Quarterly*, *16*(5), 723–47.

Beyersdorf, N. (2015). *Journey to Excellence* [Slideshare]. Retrieved from https://www.slideshare.net/optimaltransformation/an-organizations-journey-to-excellence-begins-once-it-ceases-to-sacrifice-quality-for-speed-neil-beyersdorf

Hoyte, D. S., and Greenwood, R. A. (2007). Journey to the North Face: A guide to business transformation. *Academy of Strategic Management Journey*, *6*, 91–104.

Tichy, N. M., and Devanna, M. A. (1987). Review: The transformational leader. *The Academy of Management Executive*, *1*(1), 74–76.

Weiner, J. (n.d.). Top 8 Quotes by Jeff Weiner [AZ Quotes]. Retrieved June 23, 2017, from http://www.azquotes.com/author/31965-Jeff_Weiner

CHAPTER 3: BUY-IN

Farmer, B. A., Slater, J. W., and Wright, K. S. (1998). The role of communication in achieving shared vision under new organizational leadership. *Journal of Public Relations Research*, *10*(4), 219–35.

Parish, J. T., Cadwallader, S., and Busch, P. (2008). Want to, need to, out to: Employee commitment to organizational change. *Journal of Organizational Change Management*, *21*(1), 32–52.

CHAPTER 4: EMPOWERMENT

Coquyt, M., and Creasman, B. (2017). *Growing Leaders Within: A Process Toward Teacher Leadership*. Lanham, MD: Rowman and Littlefield Publishers.

Freire, C., and Fernandes, A. (2015). Search for trustful leadership in secondary schools. *Educational Management Administration and Leadership*, *44*(6), 892–916.

GanijiNia, H., Gilaninia, S., Sharami, R., and PoorAli, M. (2013). Over of employees: Empowerment in organizations. *Business and Management Review*, *3*(2), 38–43.

Nixon, B. (1994). Facilitating empowerment in organizations. *Leadership and Organization Development Journal*, *15*(4), 3.

Yuki, G. A., and Becker, W. S. (2006). Effective empowerment in organizations. *Organization Management Journal*, *3*(3), 46–69.

CHAPTER 5: CHANGE

Adserias, R. P., Charleston, L. J., and Jackson, J. F. (2017). What style of leadership is best suited to direct organizational change to fuel institutional diversity in higher education? *Race Ethnicity and Education, 20*(3), 315–31.

Carter, L., Goldsmith, M., Smallwood, N., Sullivan, R. L., and Ulrich, D. (2013). *The Change Champion's Field Guide: Strategies and Tools for Leading.* Greensboro, NC: The Center for Creative Leadership.

Goodman, E., and Loh, L. (2012). Organizational change. *Business Information Review, 28*(4), 242–50.

Hall, G. E., and Hord, S. M. (1987). *Change in Schools: Facilitating the Process.* Albany, NY: State University of New York Press.

CHAPTER 6: CAPACITY

Chuang, S. F. (2013). Essential skills for leadership effectiveness in diverse workplace development. *Online Journal for Workforce Education and Development, 6*(1), 1–23.

Feeney, E. J. (2009). Taking a look at a school's leadership capacity: The role and function of high school department chairs. *Clearing House, 82*(5), 212–18.

King, M. B., and Bouchard, K. (2011). The capacity to build organizational capacity in schools. *Journal of Educational Administration, 49*(6), 653–69.

Sigurðardóttir, S. M., and Sigþórsson, R. (2015). The fusion of school improvement and leadership capacity in an elementary school. *Educational Management Administration and Leadership, 44*(4), 599–616.

CHAPTER 7: EXECUTION

Fogg, C. D. (1999). *Implementing your strategic plan: How to turn "intent" into effective action for sustainable change.* New York: AMACOM.

Nelson, S. S. (2009). *Implementing for Results: Your Strategic Plan in Action.* Chicago, IL: American Library Association.

Nutt, P. C. (1989). Selecting tactics to implement strategic plans. *Strategic Management Journal, 10*(2), 145.

Steel, R., and Young, E. (1991). Implementing the Corporate Strategic Plan. *Business Quarterly, 55*(3), 119.

Wheeland, C. M. (2016). Implementing a Community-wide Strategic Plan. *American Review of Public Administration, 33*(1), 46–69.

Yohn, D.L.(2012, August 14). Excuse me, could someone please explain strategy? [Blog Post]. Retrieved from http://bulldogdummond.com/blog/excuse-me-could-someone-please-explain-the-strategy

CHAPTER 8: SUSTAINABILITY

Bass, P., and Rubin, J. (2012). Sustainability of change. *Policy and Practice*, *70*(3), 19, 51.

Brannmark, M., and Benn, S. (2012). A proposed model for evaluating the sustainability of continuous change programmes. *Journal of Change Management*, *12*(2), 231–45.

Greenhalgh, T., MacFarlane, F., Barton-Sweeney, C., and Woodard, F. (2012). If we build it, Will it Stay? A Case Study of the Sustainability of Whole-System Change in London. *Milbank Quarterly*, *90*, 516–47.

About the Authors

Brian Creasman, EdD, is currently superintendent of Fleming County Schools in Kentucky. He has served as an assistant superintendent, a high school and middle school principal and assistant principal, and an instructional technologist and classroom teacher. He is the co-author of *The Leader Within: Understanding and Empowering Teacher Leaders* and *Growing Leaders Within: A Process toward Teacher Leadership.*

Jesse Bacon is the newly appointed superintendent of Bullitt County Schools in Kentucky and is working toward an EdD in educational leadership at the University of Kentucky. He previously served as the principal of Simons Middle School in Fleming County, Kentucky. Jesse has participated in numerous leadership programs, including the Leadership Institute for School Principals through the Center for Creative Leadership (CCL), the National Institute for School Leaders (NISL) Executive Development Program, as well as the American Association of School Administrators (AASA) Aspiring Superintendents Academy. He has also presented at numerous conferences on school leadership and is an active participant on Advanc-ED school and district accreditation teams.

David Franklin, EdD, is a professor of education for National University and an educational consultant for schools across the country. He has served as a primary and secondary school principal, as well as a classroom teacher. He has published articles in the *New York Academy of Public Education Professional Journal* as well as in publications in India and the Middle East. His articles published on the website "The Principal's Desk" have been downloaded a quarter of a million times by educators across the world.